RESPONSES TO INDUSTRIALISATION

The British Experience 1780–1850

Malcolm I. Thomis

DAVID & CHARLES
Newton Abbot   London   Vancouver
ARCHON BOOKS
Hamden, Connecticut
1976

To Keith and Edna Train

This edition first published in 1976 in Great Britain by David & Charles (Publishers) Limited, Newton Abbot, Devon, in Canada by Douglas David & Charles Limited, 1875 Welch Street, North Vancouver BC, and in the United States of America by Archon Books, an imprint of The Shoe String Press, Inc, Hamden, Connecticut 06514

ISBN 0 7153 6762 5 (Great Britain)

Library of Congress Cataloging in Publication Data

Thomis, Malcolm I.
    Responses to industrialisation

    Includes bibliographical references and index.
    1. Great Britain—Social conditions—19th century. 2. Great Britain—Social conditions—18th century. 3. Great Britain—Industries. I. Title.
HN385.T444   301.24'3'0941   75-45331
ISBN 0-208-01588-4 (Archon)

Set in eleven on thirteen point Baskerville and printed in Great Britain by Latimer Trend & Company Ltd Plymouth

Contents

By the same author

THE LUDDITES

1 The Industrial Revolution and Contemporary Awareness

Amongst the great changes that have transformed man's condition through the centuries of recorded history none has been so fundamental or far-reaching in its effects as the Industrial Revolution. It is not surprising then that this great complex of developments should have been the subject of an almost infinite range of controversies concerning its causes and consequences, or that there should be arguments about the naming of this incredible progeny of the human race, born in Great Britain at some unagreed time in the eighteenth century. The French are said to have called it 'The Industrial Revolution' because they believed that economic changes taking place across the Channel paralleled their own political experiences, and Robert Owen was allegedly the first native Briton to employ the term, though it was Arnold Toynbee in the 1880s who made it popular and supplied many of the emotional overtones that are still associated with the title.

The precise history of the name and its suitability for the owner are, however, less important than the generally agreed list of changes that it comprehends, for wherever any one individual might choose to place his emphasis he would be compelled to recognise that the Industrial Revolution embraced profound change in many aspects of life and activity. Some people would wish to emphasise the population explosion which transformed these sparsely populated islands of a few million people into an over-crowded and densely packed community, and they would associate with this the population redistribution which converted people from country-dwellers into town-dwellers. The growth of the towns, the replacement of a rural by an urban civilisation, had enormous implications for the physical landscape, and for some the process of industrialisation is concerned above all with changes in the countryside. For others, changes in society are what really mattered, and the social causes and consequences of the Industrial Revolution demand their main attention. The growth of industry and changes in its structure and location are also very central processes; the mechanical revolution, the application of power of various kinds, the destruction of the domestic system, the location of industry in factories, the location of factories in towns, the transport facilities required by the new industry, all these changes transform an economy as well as a countryside and a way of life, all of them interconnect, all of these, and more besides, are part of what people understand when they talk of the Industrial Revolution. And they can understand so much by it and see so many ramifications in each particular item because they are separated from these times of intensive change by almost two centuries, a separation which has allowed experience to accumulate, stock-taking to occur, and judgment to mature.

It is, of course, impossible that contemporaries, without these advantages, should have seen so much or so clearly. They possessed the ability to forecast neither future events nor the future verdicts of history writers, and the most that can reasonably be expected is that they should have revealed some degree of perception, experienced some slight apprehension of the processes of major economic and social change, some hint of the uniqueness of what they were witnessing. Some would be more perceptive than others and would be aware of relationships that others as yet could not see, and it is this rare insight that rewards the search. More than this it would be unreasonable to hope for and impossible to find.

It is important to enquire precisely what they did see, in part because strange claims have been made about the extreme perspicacity of characters in history and their ability to assimilate what was happening around them or even to prophesy future events. For instance, a suggestion that the parliamentary classes became aware in the 1760s that the Industrial Revolution was about to happen and accordingly took steps to ensure that the workers remained under close control, must surely rate as a piece of unhistorical thinking.[1] Nor is it easy to accept another claim that people must have been aware of the Industrial Revolution because there was so much evidence around that they could not fail to see it.[2] For evidence to be absorbed and assimilated so quickly would have required the most acute observation, understanding, and foresight. Adam Smith, the author of *Wealth of Nations*, published in 1776, was for long regarded as the great prophet of the Industrial Revolution because his treatise on commerce contained ideas which were to prove so relevant to the later expansion of trade and industry, but it can be fairly convincingly demonstrated that he had little idea of the industrial changes that were about to happen.[3] And William Pitt the Younger must also be dethroned from his seat of prophecy where he once supposedly sat, plotting and planning the financial and administrative measures necessary to facilitate the birth of the new industrial economy.

Apart from the exposure of such anachronisms, there is another reason why it is important to assess contemporary awareness. Arguably, what was in fact happening will always prove in the end to be more important than what people thought was happening, yet in the short term the imagined occurrences might well determine response and motivate action. If it is desirable to know, for instance, to what extent early nineteenth-century social protest was a more or less deliberate revolt against industrialisation, it is certainly necessary to know how far and in what ways the processes of industrialisation were being experienced. Methodologically this presents some problems. It would, of course, be a mistake to suppose that people's words and actions represent the totality of their thoughts, or that there was always someone on hand to record them, but this is always the historian's problem. He must proceed with what he has and not with what he would like to have.

If the whole complex of changes and relationships involved in the concept of Industrial Revolution were not and could not have been appreciated by contemporaries, many of the component parts certainly were, and of these the easiest to recognise were the physical changes, the growing towns, the greater number of people, the factories, and the machines. Each could in turn be recognised, even if its precise relationship to all the rest could not.

The new towns were a widely observed phenomenon of the late eighteenth century, and contemporaries had little difficulty in attributing their appearance and growth to what they called 'manufactures'. There were innumerable references to the populous manufacturing towns which had sprung into existence or risen from next to nothing to places of great size and importance with startling rapidity. Macclesfield, reported one witness in 1818, had increased by two thirds since 1786, when the silk trade had been introduced into the town, and the amazing 1811 census figures for Manchester were explained in terms of the influx of new hands, especially female, employed in spinning, weaving, fustian-cutting, and the making of umbrellas and braces.[4] New industry meant new towns, and Engels in 1844, after three more decades experience of industrial growth, was able to contrast the newer parts of the town with the remnants of the old Manchester which belonged to the days 'before the town became industrialised'.[5] The phenomenal growth of Manchester—almost six times larger in 1831 than sixty years earlier—was recorded at every stage, for this was the 'metropolis of the commercial system', 'the greatest manufacturing emporium in the world'.[6] But other centres also made a big impression. When Mr Balwhidder left his rural parish to visit Glasgow in 1791, he noticed 'a visible increase in the city, loftier buildings on all sides, and streets that spread their arms far into the embraces of the country'.[7] Similarly, Leeds, twenty-four years later, representing other branches of the textile trade, was said to astonish occasional visitors with the increase of buildings that testified to its fast-growing prosperity.[8] And size was not the only characteristic that provoked wonderment, for it was Birmingham's breadth and versatility that were commented upon by the factory commissioners in 1833 when they referred to a recent enumeration of over two hundred separate and distinct manufactures that gave employment to the workers of that town.[9] Manchester, Glasgow, Birmingham, Leeds, and Liverpool, whose 98% growth in the period 1801–31 was more than double the national average, were the eye-catching, star performers, but the smaller places were also noted.[10] As early as 1790, for instance, the Hon John Byng observed on his travels through Stockport that whereas, in 1780, 700 houses had been sufficient to accommodate the townsfolk, now more than 2,000 were proving insufficient, since the 'warmth of the cotton trade' had been felt.[11]

Urbanisation could be seen clearly: its perpetuation and extension could not. The existence of the 'rich and unrepresented towns of Leeds, Sheffield, Halifax, and Manchester' was used as an additional argument to strengthen the case of the parliamentary reformers in 1785, but neither then nor in 1832 did anyone detect a general problem which required a radical solution.[12] Similarly in local government, specific anomalies were identified but no general one. Manchester was by 1819, as Lord Folkestone told Parliament, an immense town grown from a paltry village, yet it still retained its original governmental structure, which was operated with great partiality.[13] The great unincorporated towns and the extension of others beyond the limits of corporate authority would eventually compel attention to specific needs, but the reform of the municipal corporations in 1835 was carried out with a strange lack of reference to the social changes involved in industrialisation and the administrative changes that they had necessitated. The reports of the commissioners are oddly out of touch with the ongoing process of change, and contain some surprisingly inept observations and forecasts. Amongst the towns of Yorkshire, they found Doncaster to be a market town with little likelihood of any change in its condition, York a declining place with not much prospect of improvement, and Hull, with its commercial and shipping interests, in decline and without much probability of recovery. There were no railways or steamships in their crystal ball.

Town growth was supported by population growth, though it took the census enumerations from 1801 onwards to demonstrate the overall increase of population as well as its redistribution. But even the censuses had their sceptics. Henry Brougham, a man of the highest intelligence, was unable to comprehend in 1812 how the population of the country could have undergone such a surprising increase over the previous decade in view of losses through war and emigration.[15] William Cobbett, with his strong but different kind of intellect, could not perceive in the late 1820s how any rational man could doubt that England at the time of the Plantagenets was out of all comparison more populous than it had become in this age of empty churches and depopulated commons.[16] Where overall increase was not doubted, it was certainly not understood, and this is by no means surprising in view of the perplexities that still arise from the subject, and people were much readier to comment upon and explain the more easily intelligible redistribution of population that was taking place. This they did largely in terms of the migration of agricultural labourers into industry and the influx of immigrant Irish. These were the believed sources of the population increase in Manchester, which was allegedly 186,098 in 1821 and ten years later almost half as many again.[17] In July, 1834, following the work of the Poor Law Commissioners, an office was opened in Manchester to handle the migration of labourers from the agricultural south and attempt to place them in manufacturing jobs.[18] This was a visible sign of one alleged purpose of the commissioners—to provide industry with cheap labour—but their reports had suggested a greater concern for high poor rates and the 'moral' condition of the poor than with economic growth and labour supply.

Glasgow, said to have 30,000 people in 1790, was believed to contain more than a quarter of a million in 1838, and of these one fifth were said to be natives, two fifths Lowland immigrants, one fifth Highlanders, and one fifth Irish.[19] The last group were an easily recognisable and identifiable sign of increase, and were readily blamed for the social problems of the period. From 1799 they were believed to have flooded into the west of Scotland, pulling down the native dwellers to their own standards of existence by their readiness to accept and ability to survive on lower wages. Scottish weavers maintained in 1834 that the injury done to them by 50,000 Irishmen was as great as that inflicted by the power-loom, a perceptive appreciation that their depressed state was not simply, or even principally, the consequence of mechanisation—a view that historians would confirm—though they were not able to anticipate the later realisation of the extent to which the pace of technological change was itself determined by the availability of cheap labour.[20] In Lancashire an identical story was told of floods of immigrants, given easy admission by cheap steam navigation, with disastrous consequences for the weaving trade in general and the social conditions of the large towns of Liverpool and Manchester in particular. Immigrants provided the manufacturers with an easy scapegoat and alibi whenever accusing fingers were pointed in their direction.[21]

But it was not only the textile areas that brought people together. The Mining Commissioners reported in 1844 how Coatbridge and Airdrie, for instance, in a previously remote and thinly-peopled area of the country, had increased in population with 'unexampled rapidity' after the introduction of hot-blast smelting.[22] And if industry of all kinds was capable of working this miracle, it must be remembered too, what contemporaries largely failed to see and what the Poor Law Commissioners had to remind them of in 1834—that population increase was a characteristic of purely agricultural districts as well as of the manufacturing counties.[23] Important as that is, it cannot be denied that when the first comparative figures were

13

available to Parliament, after the second census of 1811, it was Lancashire in England and Lanarkshire in Scotland that stood out pre-eminently as the great growth areas, and it was the cotton trade which, as Sir Robert Peel the Elder had said in 1806, had given birth to a whole new race of men.[24] How these new men, along with the older ones, were distributed between town and countryside remained a slightly controversial subject, in part because of the problem of establishing agreed categories. One opponent of the Corn Laws argued in 1837 that the proportion of town labourers to agricultural ones was 2:1, and he was largely supported by the Health of Towns Commissioners who reported that a 1:2 ratio in 1790 had almost been reversed by 1840.[25] Yet another MP used the 1831 census to argue that the real agricultural interest of Great Britain and Ireland must stand at twenty-one million, since the manufacturing export trades employed at the most three million people, from which he drew the not surprising conclusion that the Corn Laws should remain.[26]

Even before the new manufacturing towns began to loom large, the early factories had been a visible portent of quickening economic growth, and there was little chance of people being unaware of them. They made their immediate visual impact in the country valleys of Derbyshire and Nottinghamshire, the villages of the West Country and of Yorkshire, as well as the villages and small towns of Lancashire. A modern belief that they struck terror into the hearts of the ordinary village craftsmen is well supported by the evidence given before the early textile committees of enquiry and by the difficulties experienced by the first mills in recruiting a free labour force, difficulties which threw them back upon the expedient of employing pauper apprentices.[27] Richard Arkwright's first steam factory was erected in Manchester in 1783 and the event duly recorded by a local historian.[28] In 1788, five years before his slightly disturbing visit to Glasgow, Mr Balwhidder had observed the erection of a cotton mill in his parish; 'a spacious fabric it was', and 'nothing like it had been seen before in our day and generation.'[29] Arnold, too, a village to the north of Nottingham, had its economic and social life considerably disturbed by the erection of Davison and Hawksley's large worsted mill, which advertised in October 1794 for families to work and live there; the bigger the families, the more welcome they would be, and there were houses ready for them to which their goods would be transported free of charge.[30] An old or a small community must have been transformed by such an innovation. In 1816 the rector of Keighley, in the West Riding, reported that by 1811 his small town of 6,864 people already had 29 mills, though there had been none before 1780.[31]

Sometimes the factories appeared almost too quickly to count and comprehend. James Stuart, the Scottish factory inspector, reported in 1839 the case of a 'ten hour' advocate who had stated his belief that there were 38 factories in Glasgow when there were in fact 103.[32] Some people were so conscious of the rapid rate of factory-building, that they telescoped the whole process; for instance the Earl of Rosslyn notified Parliament in 1819 that the first cotton-spinning mill was built in 1792, and Sir Robert Peel the Elder, who really should have known better, reported that Manchester's first steam factory had been built in 1791.[33]

Another interesting reaction to factory-building was the comforting illusion which allowed some people to believe that the factories were only going to supplement the domestic system of manufacture and not replace it. This is strongly evident in the report of the Committee on Woollen Manufactures in 1806 and in the attitude of William Wilberforce, one of the Yorkshire MPs.[34] These people were movingly eloquent on the superior virtues of the domestic system, and protested vigorously that they would not tolerate those developments that promoted factory growth if there was the remotest possibility that these might threaten the old ways of production. As late as 1845 an official commission was still quoting with approval the opinions of the Nottingham lace merchant and statistician, William Felkin, that the factory system was still in its infancy

15

and that there was no reason to believe that all weaving must necessarily be done in factories.[35] In a strict sense this was true, though it was also a highly misleading comment. Felkin would continue to idealise the way of life and independent character of his grandfather, 'the stout-hearted weaver', but even the stocking knitters were moving into factories when he produced his biographical study, *The Stout-hearted Weaver*, in 1872.

New factories had been necessary to house new machines as T. S. Ashton's celebrated 'wave of gadgets' swept over the country in the second half of the eighteenth century.[36] The early textile inventions, such as Kay's flying shuttle and the spinning-jenny of Hargreaves, had made no difference to the domestic structure of industry in setting the cotton trade in motion, but Arkwright's water-frame demanded first that it should be sited by running water and later where steam power could be conveniently mobilised, and this had meant factories. Even the domestic inventions provoked anti-machine riots, and both Hargreaves and Arkwright were driven from their native Lancashire to find a more hospitable reception in Nottingham. But the anti-machine phase passed quickly and resistance to technological change did not remain prominent in cotton-worker attitudes. Amongst other classes, the new machinery was widely seen as the key to industrial progress and has indeed remained foremost in the popular image of the Industrial Revolution and its causes, despite scholars' inclination to see invention as the daughter of necessity and social pressure rather than the mother of industry.[37] As early as 1785 Arkwright's achievement in spinning was already hailed as 'the most admirable invention that ever was produced and brought to perfection by the ingenuity and perseverance of any one man.'[38] It prompted the complementary invention of the power-loom, patented by Cartwright in 1786, though not in general use until the 1820s, and was itself improved upon by Crompton's mule and later the self-actor, which the *Manchester Guardian* immediately realised was 'destined to work a complete revolution in the mode of spinning cotton'.[39] But Arkwright had made the

16

great breakthrough, and it was the coming together of his invention with the other great invention of the period, Watt's steam-engine, that in 1783 gave James Ogden of Manchester so momentous an event to record in Miller's Lane, for here it was 'that Mr Arkwright's machines are setting to work by a steam-engine for the carding and spinning of cotton'.[40]

In terms of frequency of contemporary references, Arkwright and Watt were the best known inventors of the age, and if Arkwright was believed to be at the bottom of the great commercial growth of the age, it was the application of Watt's steam-engine that soon became the measure of industrial growth and progress in particular areas. It was, for instance, a source of considerable satisfaction to the editor of the *Leeds Mercury*, in May 1830, that the parish of Leeds now housed 231 steam-engines, which was not unreasonably interpreted as a sign of the recent great increase in the manufacturing trades of the area.[41] The steam-engines above all other inventions attracted the foreign visitors on their British tours, and when they could gain access to workshops, whose owners lived in perpetual fear of industrial espionage, they delighted in recording the many and ingenious purposes which they were being made to serve. Dr Spiker, the librarian to the King of Prussia, toured the country in 1816 and left a record of the almost infinite variety of uses to which they were put. He observed steam-engines at work preparing clay for making china in Worcester, rolling sheets of copper, stretching gold and silver plate, glass-grinding, and wire-drawing in Birmingham, in addition to manufacturing iron-hooks for Waterloo medals and boring cylinders to make—other steam-engines! In the Potteries they were grinding stones to clay, sifting and turning pottery; in Leeds pulling coal-waggons and finishing cloth; on Tyneside blowing bellows in the iron-works and operating two enormous hammers; in the coalmines of Morpeth pumping water from the shaft and drawing up the baskets of coal; operating power-looms in Glasgow, and all species of cotton-machinery in Preston; and hauling up containers of salt from the salt-mines of Northwich.[42] The industrial processes of early nineteenth century Britain were clearly seen as being vitally dependent on the inventive observations of James Watt, even if the business enterprise required to put steam-engines into production was not something to which contemporaries were able to attribute a similar kind of importance.

New machines in new factories in new towns meant commercial expansion, and it was the great increase in trade, rather than the growth of industry as such, that made the first impression on the rulers of the land in the eighteenth century. William Pitt the Younger delighted in the progress of cotton manufacture in the 1780s because this would promote trade, described by a contemporary in Parliament as 'the true majesty of Great Britain'.[43] And to promote trade he pursued good, old-fashioned policies of trying to dominate overseas markets for British products, policies which were liberalised a little by the infusion of some notions of freer trade which he had inherited from Adam Smith. The means were slightly changed, but the ends remained the same; extended commerce, said Pitt in 1787, would advance maritime strength, and the message was spelled out even more clearly by Lord Stanhope in 1814—if our manufactures were injured, our commerce would be injured and we should then lose our only sure foundation, the strength and glory of the navy.[44] And events seemed to be favouring Britain, for witnesses were able to tell a parliamentary committee of enquiry in 1803 how it was generally understood that Britain had captured the market of the world since the French Revolution, that the French troubles had opened up Russia to her, and that trade had doubled in consequence of these events.[45] Three years later another committee reported a rapid and prodigious increase in commerce which was universally known to have taken place.[46] That such a commercial dominance might be more easily achieved by unrestricted trade than by tariff wars was appreciated by ministers and by MPs long before they appreciated that commerce was now required to serve a quite different purpose in national life. Anachronistic concepts of developing manufactures in order to promote trade and maritime strength, instead of promoting trade in order to encourage industry, seem strangely mercantilist for the beginnings of this free trade era. Manufacturing was still being seen as a means of fostering trade and building up national strength rather than as a way of life for an ever-increasing proportion of the people. Manufacturing industries were transforming the country, and hardly anyone realised in the early years of the nineteenth century that this was happening.

The growth of cotton in particular was not seen for what it was—an agent of radical economic and social change whose influence would permeate almost all aspects of the economy and society. The industry was known to have expanded by leaps and bounds after the Versailles Peace of 1783, so that by 1785 the Manchester manufactures were said by one MP to be the pride of the country and the envy of foreign nations, a pride which gave employment to 40,000 Lancashire workers.[47] Two years later Lord Hawksley paid fulsome tribute to the industry, for almost every article within it had already been brought to a state of perfection despite being of very recent innovation.[48] The Hon John Byng described it as 'the now overspread cotton trade' during his travels of 1790; its influence had reached as far south as Leicester, a spread which he had cause to lament, though he was compelled to admit that it both populated and enriched the areas it now encompassed.[49] And the alleged £1 million of cotton exports of 1791 were to leap to an incredible £9¾ million by 1807 and to constitute one third of the country's total exports.[50] It would be difficult to disagree with the view of Kirkman Finlay, MP and cotton manufacturer, expressed in 1818, that cotton was the most important manufacture ever established in the country.[51] People sang its praises and were right to comment on its outstanding achievement. Yet what they were observing was not something that was simply the best yet, but something that was quite different in kind from its predecessors and something that would have immeasurably more far-reaching consequences than anything that had gone before it. In other words they missed the uniqueness of what was happening around them, which was not altogether surprising; what they identified as merely a quantitative change was in fact a qualitative change that had so far gone undetected. The economic miracle that cotton was working in the economy could only be seen at a distance, though its social consequences would be more immediately evident.[52]

On the causes of industrial expansion the quality of observation was similarly limited by the nearness of events. A perceptive analysis of Manchester's rise was made by one of its residents James Ogden, in 1783, in terms of the ingenuity of its mechanics; the large amount of capital accumulated and invested in the area; the development of a strong export trade in calico printing which forced production; the introduction of machinery, especially in spinning; and the advantages of Manchester's unincorporated status, which permitted the free access of strangers to the town without the restrictions and regulations they might have encountered elsewhere.[53] Apart from his amusing, and not irrational, rejection of the idea of a charter of incorporation or parliamentary representation for Manchester —the latter because elections would interfere with work— Ogden's points of emphasis were to receive much support elsewhere. In particular his stress on machinery helped to initiate the most dominant theme of contemporary explanations of British success. Fifty years later, in 1836, the manufacturer, John Fielden, produced an almost text-book model answer on why Lancashire had featured so prominently. He identified the geographical position, the natural resources, and the climate so regularly cited by later generations of schoolchildren, to which he added the dexterity and superiority of the workpeople and their superior machines, advantages which, he believed, England would always possess.[54] Through all her advantages Lancashire had, in the words of Edward Baines, discovered the art of making gold without the alchemist's art, making both standing waters and flowing streams subservient to her prosperity.[55]

Some help too had been received from the accidents of war, or the 'circumstances of that eventful period' as the *Leeds Mercury* had put it, though the precise contribution of the French wars to Britain's success was more readily seen shortly afterwards than at the time.[56] By the chances of war, wrote William Howitt in 1838, Britain had begun to manufacture and farm for the whole world and on her own terms; this had forced a vast working population into existence.[57] At the time, the manufacturers were not so ready to concede that the wars had placed them in a favoured position. In September, 1809, the *Nottingham Review* had asked why the country should be intending to celebrate the golden jubilee of George III, when his reign had plunged the nation into such irretrievable difficulties, and the Luddite crisis of 1811–12 made manufacturers much more conscious of the commercial distress arising from the continental blockade and the American interdict than of the opportunities being opened up to them.[58] At the end of the war the *Review* estimated that the trading and manufacturing interests had suffered privations and losses over the previous twenty years unequalled at any period in history.[59] Still, the *Manchester Mercury* admitted in October 1816, that the transition from war to peace had caused distress and stagnation of trade, an implicit concession that war had not been without its compensations, which were soon to be widely understood, if not by Nottingham's hosiers and the manufacturers.[60]

Another aspect of causation which was exemplified in contemporary thought was a growing appreciation of the links between different aspects of industrial expansion, and the cumulative effects of changes in different parts of the economy. This was the beginning of a shrewder appraisal of the cause and course of growth. One such sign was a report in the *Manchester Mercury*, in April 1800, of the opening of the Peak Forest Canal, uniting the Peak of Derbyshire with the populous parts of Lancashire. This transport innovation made possible the carriage of manufactured goods from out of Lancashire and lime and limestone into Lancashire, where it was needed for the building demanded by industrial progress, and for road construction—a further transport innovation necessitated by the growth of manufactures.[61] Similarly, in 1805 the paper remarked on the opening of the Liverpool to Hull canal link, and the coal and other important commodities which were already beginning to pass through.[62] This inter-connection was shrewdly highlighted by Dr Spiker in 1816, who had by then been able to observe not only the rise but also the decline of the Shropshire iron trade whose employed labour force of 3,000 had, he said, been reduced to a mere 300 by the rise of the Carron Co of Falkirk, which had been able to capture the London trade as a result of the canal network that was now available for its use.[63] Comments and observations were becoming more sophisticated. In July 1836, the *Manchester Guardian* described attempts that were being made to establish cotton manufacture in Hull, and listed the assets on which Hull could draw, but rightly emphasised the Yorkshire town's inability to call upon a local skilled labour force of a kind that Manchester then enjoyed in abundance.[64] And in 1842 the Commissioners on Children's Employment were noting not only the great variety of occupations that had developed in Birmingham, but were also appreciating, as later historians of Chartism, for instance, were to emphasise, the advantages that this gave to its people by allowing them to escape the commercial convulsions that caused periodic distress in Lancashire where the towns were so heavily dependent on cotton.[65]

In some of these comments can be detected the beginnings of realisation that the many facets of industrialisation were interconnected. They all naturally fell far short of T. S. Ashton's masterly appraisal in 1948 which rejected monocausal explanations and in one sentence identified the following factors— growing supplies of land, labour, and capital which permitted the expansion of industry, coal and steam which provided the fuel and power, and low rates of interest, rising prices and high expectations of profit which offered the necessary incentive.[66] Scholars might disagree over the emphasis they would give to particular ingredients in the mix, and the timing or even the location of the vital changes, but they would be nearly unanimous about the complexities of the problem, and ready enough to sympathise with early faltering attempts to explain the almost inexplicable.

Over the period 1780–1840 there was a wide realisation that unprecedented growth was taking place in terms of national wealth, population, towns, industrial expansion production techniques, and transport, and some attempts were made to explain this growth. What people failed to realise, through no fault of their own, was the result of these changes—that these individual achievements were adding up to something that would later be identified as a revolution within society of perhaps unparalleled importance. The occasional insight can be detected. There was for instance an awareness that times were changing and strange things happening in Byng's injunction to his 'poor deluded country' in 1790 to 'strain away in trade; enclose, depopulate, build towns; pull down villages; and deal away so wildly that we all become swindlers and bankrupts.'[67] The pace and the madness and the content alarmed him. Not so the future financier, Vansittart, who saw in 1794 'signs of eminent felicity existing in the nation beyond all former example', signs exemplified in public works and buildings, cultivation of the land, and the growth of shipping, capital, and property in general; for him these were welcome developments, and his forecasts were to be substantiated in the nineteenth century verdicts on these years.[68] The accumulation of capital over the past thirty-six years, reported the *Manchester Guardian* in 1833, was without parallel in the history of the world, and the nation flourished as never before.[69] More progress had been made in half a century, it reported the following year, than in any previous half century in the nation's history, for, as Howitt was to write in 1838, there was no nation to compare with England.[70] The national existence had been much changed and there remained promise of changes too vast to be readily imagined. In modern parlance, the Industrial Revolution was by

1838, well advanced. But only thirteen years earlier, in 1825, William Huskisson had given to Parliament a useful but thoroughly conventional and unimaginative recital of British achievements, relating the growth of cotton, invention, capital, and industry, but using them only to explain Britain's commanding position in the world.[71] He was evidently not thinking of an industrial society but of a traditional one with valuable manufacturing districts within it which would enable the nation to fulfil more successfully its traditional aims. It was the Pitt concept encountered earlier.

Perhaps the most perceptive of contemporary observers, the first to realise that a change in kind rather than a change in degree was occurring, was Robert Owen, the first critic of industrial society. Not only did Owen see that in the half century, 1770–1822, Britain had experienced scientific improvement and technological change beyond that of all other countries—in the steam-engine and spinning machinery in particular—and that her productive power had been increased more than twelve-fold, but he also appreciated that an irreversible process of industrialisation had been set in motion which was altering the very character of the mass of the people of the country.[72] That he should have diagnosed the existence of a new society is more important than either his condemnation of the evils of this new society or his belief that ultimately good would result when the new forces were properly controlled. This kind of observation is of a quality rarely encountered in the first three decades of the nineteenth century.

Another person who had some glimmer of the magnitude of occurring changes was Macaulay, who defended parliamentary reform in 1831 on the grounds that a great revolution had taken place, new forms of property and new portions of society come into existence, yet new people were still living under old institutions.[73] This brilliant analysis exposed the general anomaly within the political system, unlike the nit-picking efforts of Russell and other advocates of reform, who concentrated on individual cases of rotten boroughs to be eliminated or large

towns to be enfranchised. But even Macaulay detracted something from his analysis by suggesting that all history was full of
similar revolutions produced by causes similar to those then
operating, thus apparently missing the unique nature of the
British experience.

Within the press, the *Manchester Guardian* combined long
stretches of almost total neglect with occasional flashes of real
insight, such as the claim, in April 1825, that the mechanical
inventions of the previous half century had produced a 'complete revolution' in transferring industry from the home to the
factory, where so much fixed capital was invested that the
manufacturer had of necessity to change his approach and employ his machinery much more intensively.[74] A reader of Manchester newspapers through the first thirty years of the nineteenth century would be hard-pressed to recognise here this
problem city which was later believed to contain all those
ingredients of social anarchy that disturbed the peace of mind
of the early Victorians. But signs of awareness were soon to
appear. The cholera epidemic of 1832, and Dr Kay's publication on the state of the working class of Manchester, provoked a
profoundly perceptive editorial on the new society and its
problems which had arisen from the new towns and the
extended manufacturing developments which they housed.[75]

Joseph Hume, in 1828, advocated a division of labour
among nations, by which British capital, manufactures, and
commerce might designate Britain's role in the world, whilst
other nations were responsible for feeding her.[76] Carlyle in 1829
identified 'industrialism', whilst factory and mines inspectors
in the 1840s apprehended the unprecedented changes that had
taken place with which the ancient institutions of the country
had simply not kept pace.[77] They began to spell out in so many
words the need to make adjustments to accommodate the new
industrial society that was coming into being. But the nineteenth
century was almost half way over before this message was
coming across clearly, and only the beginnings of its implementa-
tion had been made by 1850.

A more typical reaction of the first half of the century is that which offers some appreciation of the extent of the change, mingled with comment that betrays lack of understanding. In 1834, two West Country witnesses before the Poor Law Commissioners illustrated neatly the contrasting attitudes. One acknowledged that Gloucester woollens would never regain their former importance, and showed a good appreciation of why this should be; he even recognised that 'a new state of things has taken place which requires new laws'. The other spoke about the problems of guarding against fluctuations in the woollen trade of the West, as if the problem were simply a question of fluctuations.[78] Henry Brougham, arguably one of the most intelligent men of his day, a Whig and a product of the Scottish Enlightenment, argued in 1817 that agriculture was the ultimate source of the country's wealth and prosperity, and predicted that if peace lasted there was nothing to prevent continental countries from rivalling Britain, for he had no appreciation of Britain's unique position.[79] Michael Sadler, the friend of the factory children and parliamentary leader of the campaign for factory legislation, talked in 1831 of the period of great change in which people were then living, and said there was none to equal the revolution that had occurred in the state and condition of the agricultural poor.[80] Dr Peter Gaskell, writing in 1836, commented perceptively on how the British had changed from being an agricultural people to being a manufacturing one; but he then went on to say that neither agriculture nor manufactures could employ any further people, and that machinery would eventually render even the whole of the existing factory population redundant and unemployed.[81]

Of all such enigmatic commentators, the greatest enigma was undoubtedly William Cobbett, the champion of old England and its supposed virtues, who said so much yet saw so little. He denounced the 'lords of the loom' who had taken industry from the cottage, which they had been enabled to do by the 'funding system' and a foolish government. For him the 'funding system' was to be blamed for all things; it was fundamental.

Instead of believing that 'funding' was symptomatic of industrialisation, Cobbett actually believed the opposite, that industrialisation was a symptom of the other and greater evil. And so he could argue in 1825 that over a forty-year period all had changed for the worse for the working classes, and then go on to explain himself not in terms of industrial change but in terms of taxes, funding, and paper-money.[82]

It would be difficult to answer with any certainty the question of which groups within society contained the most accurate and perceptive observers of the process of industrialisation, whether it was the businessmen who ran the new industries, the working men who laboured within them, the Benthamite commissioners who were, after all, professional observers and investigators, who looked at many aspects of the new society and recommended changes, or perhaps even the social critics amongst writers and novelists who stood outside economic processes and were possibly able to see them more clearly by means of their distanced view. The choice of any one group might well be a fairly arbitrary matter according to where sympathies lie and according to attitudes adopted by particular groups. Some would wish, for instance, to argue that no group had a clearer experience of what industrialisation involved than the workers who bore the main burden of the new production processes, whilst others might feel that the entrepreneurs who risked their capital must surely have been more aware than any other group of the new economic and social structure, the opportunities it offered, and the risks involved in exploiting them.

It could very reasonably be argued that the statisticians who emerged in the 1830s and attempted to quantify society, its assets and its liabilities, should have been better equipped than any other group to offer mature and comprehensive judgment. Certainly John Marshall gave to the handloom weavers enquiry in 1835 a detailed, reasoned, and overall view of the course of industrial change which was quite different from the kind of evidence that they received from other witnesses. He explained in detail how the invention of particular machines, the application of steam-power, and the location of fuel resources had led to an internal migration of the population and the shift of industry from counties such as Essex, Norfolk, Suffolk, and Hampshire to Lancashire and the West Riding; and he supported his claims with the necessary statistical backing.[83] G. R. Porter, in charge of the statistical department of the Board of Trade, which was founded in 1832, was formally responsible for acquiring information on the 'Progress of the nation', which he took as the title of a book he wrote. But when faced with the task of explaining why he had chosen to start his book with the year 1800, he showed a curious neglect of the Industrial Revolution and the obvious progress arising from it. Instead he referred to the legislative union with Ireland as a good starting point, the availability of material from the census enumerations which had begun in 1801, and the neatness of the period at his command, of which a third was wartime and two thirds peace-time—convenient for the comparisons he wished to make.[84] And the census enumeration of 1801, which it would be tempting to attribute to an understandable desire on the part of an industrialising nation to take stock of its manpower resources, was undertaken primarily with reference to the food crisis of this famine period.[85] The new social scientists and the science they practised were probably as much a consequence of a growing awareness of industrialisation and its problems as they were a cause of this awareness, though their surveys of the thirties and forties undoubtedly helped to make more people aware of the problems of urbanisation and industrialisation which had brought them into being in the early thirties.

Some of the best feeling for the changes taking place can be found in the testimony of individual people who were old enough to have lived through many momentous years, and who could at least say what they had experienced and how changes had affected them personally. What they were not, of course, usually able to do was to generalise from their own experience or see bigger principles at work. Duncan Lennox, a Glasgow

weaver, commenting on the prevalent distress in 1811, informed
the enquiring committee that he had 'wrought under a uniformity of wages for near forty years'; he could remember the
stagnation of trade in 1760–1 and 1772–3, but hard work had
always enabled the men to keep their wages up until recent
years, which he recognised as a new phase for the trade, and in
this he was right.[86] Another weaver, from Bolton, told the 1834
enquiry a similar story of good wages forty years earlier which
recent times could not match.[87] The old men had a sense of
perspective as far as their own fortunes were concerned, and the
Bolton man confirmed the trends described in the 1826
weavers' appeal to the manufacturers and merchants of Manchester, which claimed as a well-known fact that wages in
weaving had been gradually going down for a period of twenty-
five years.[88] The men clearly understood that something more
than fluctuation was at work here, even if they were not quite
sure what. In 1833 a magistrate from Thetford in Norfolk,
John Wright, told the Poor Law Commissioners that he was old
enough to remember the time when every cottager possessed a
number of spinning-wheels equal to the number of his family,
when children had been introduced to the wheel at an early age
and acquired the proper virtues in consequence.[89] Whatever
opinion might be held about the man's views on what constituted the best life for children, there is no doubt that he typifies
an experience of the change which occurred over this most
dramatic period, as did the old man of Carluke in Lanarkshire
whose memories were recorded in the *Second Statistical Account of
Scotland*. Living in a village of 2,125 people, he could remember
the time when Carluke had consisted of four cottages, a kirk,
and a manse.[90]

The general impression left by the personal testimonies of
working men is that people's thoughts were largely confined to
the narrower, limited setting of their own jobs and lives rather
than concerned with any overall concept of history, and this is
not to be wondered at. The nearest that most came to any
grander view was in taking action to protest against the

Combination Laws or to limit hours of work, campaigns intimately related to their conditions of work and not necessarily implying any attitude towards industrialisation. Working-class protest up to and including Chartism, has often been interpreted as an attempt to reverse the process of industrialisation, but there is little enough evidence of any awareness of a general process amongst the working classes to justify belief in a conscious, concerted movement of resistance to it. Like their employers, the workers were essentially practical, pragmatic men concerned to remedy a grievance over wages, hours, or prices, rather than to display an attitude towards industrialisation.

And the same might also be said of the governors of Great Britain who were responsible for the affairs of the nation through these years of economic and social change. Any thought that they directed the process of industrialisation with a clarity of vision and close control must quickly be abandoned, for historians have above all been impressed by the spontaneity of the Industrial Revolution, the little it owed to conscious planning and the little assistance it received from governments. This last might be summarised as the unwitting help given over low interest rates in the eighteenth century and the consequent availability of cheap capital, and also the protection given to new industries which was a relic of the protectionist, mercantilist system and in no way derived from a new decision to assist industrialisation. From the government there was not much help and even less awareness of what was happening. Pitt's attitude, it has been seen, was traditional in its aims if slightly novel in its means, and it would be difficult to read any particular awareness into, for instance, his declared intent in 1790 to 'increase our wealth, our population, our industry, our strength, and our enterprise'.[91] Such a sentiment might have come from any national leader over the previous 150 years and hardly marks Pitt as a man apart.

A curious tale was told by a Bolton weaver in 1834 of a conversation he had held with the chief minister many years earlier, in which Pitt had, he said, forecast the course and character of industrial growth and predicted that the time might come for future governments to interfere in the relations between workmen and their employers to control the possible abuses that unscrupulous owners might introduce into industry. Such a time had arrived, claimed the weaver, and he cited Pitt's alleged attitude in support of wage regulation, the control of machinery, and other aspects of the weavers' case.[92] Had any conversation taken place between this man and William Pitt, it seems most improbable that the minister would have indulged in such prophecy, that his prophecy would have been accurate, or that he would ever have recommended such a remedy, which was quite out of line with his views on industrial relations.

And if Pitt's record on the question, distinguished above all by his Combination Laws, offers little grounds for seeing him as a friend of the emerging working classes, neither were all his policies calculated to endear him to the manufacturing interests, who were convinced in the 1780s that he was trying to stifle rather than promote industrial growth. In 1784 he defended his taxes on cotton goods on the grounds that previous duties had not checked consumption, and in 1785 argued that as the cotton trade was increasing it was, therefore, a proper object of taxation; manufacturing industries were evidently regarded as revenue-raisers for the government.[93] Such men as Pitt, argued Burke with his customary eloquence for which due allowance must be made, when in power converted large cities into small villages, which was hardly a prescription for industrial growth.[94] The Irish commercial proposals evoked 'fear and apprehension' amongst manufacturers, which Pitt had to recognise even though he believed it to be far-fetched and ill-founded, whilst going to war with France in 1793 was bitterly opposed in the manufacturing towns because of the damage that it was expected to bring to trade and industry.[95] For half a century Lancashire merchants and manufacturers petitioned for the abolition of the duty on raw cotton, and a similar running war existed between the government and the Yorkshire woollen manufacturers. This reached a climax in 1824 when the government was widely denounced for retaining taxes on the import of raw wool, and at the same time proposing to allow the free export of long wool in order to placate the wool growers, the landed interest. The government was thus, according to the *Leeds Mercury*, allowing foreign rivals a duty-free raw material whilst denying it to British manufacturers.[96] The special pleading of manufacturing interests is notorious, but there is plenty of evidence to suggest that they felt successive governments out of harmony with their industrial interests. This 'formidable combination of landowners and ministers of the crown against manufacturers', so identified by the *Nottingham Review* in 1815, was seen to be exercising its most baneful influence over the issue of the Corn Laws, which again provoked half a century of opposition before the manufacturers prevailed.[97] It is clearly arguable that industrialisation went ahead in spite, rather than because, of the government's contribution.

The passing of the great Reform Bill of 1832, which in retrospect has the appearances of a rational overhaul of the mechanisms of the system of representation to meet the strains imposed upon the system by the social changes of the Industrial Revolution, in fact illustrates the limited extent of contemporary awareness. In February 1830, Lord John Russell argued that wool, cotton, and iron ought to have their 'interests' represented in Parliament, and so he introduced a bill to give seats to Manchester, Birmingham, and Leeds. Instead of arguing that recent social change required an overall look at the political system, he took a practical and very limited look, employing the traditional argument of 'interests' to be represented as he might earlier have defended the West Indian sugar planters, the East Indian, or the Army 'interest' in the eighteenth century House of Commons.[98] In May of that year he added the silk trades and 'shipping business' to his existing list of unrepresented interests, and in June 1831 the mining districts and Potteries were added as requiring to have their claims duly regarded.[99] On each occasion Russell picked out specific abuses to eliminate from the unreformed system and specific additions that needed to be made. He defended each item he proposed, pragmatically justifying each step, without making any generalisations; there was no question of radical change to meet a totally new situation. The government's case throughout the reform crisis depended on the joke situations that ministers were able to cite of disappearing constituencies and non-existent electors, and an abortive search for references to a new social situation serves only to strengthen the appreciation of how tinkering and conservative a piece of legislation the first Reform Act really was.

It would not then be unreasonable to conclude that during the classic period of Industrial Revolution, the late decades of the eighteenth and the early decades of the nineteenth century, there were very many people who realised that great changes were taking place, for this they could hardly fail to notice, but there were very few who had any perception of the real nature of these changes. It took later generations, with the help of historians, to appreciate this, which was perhaps very natural and very proper.

Notes to this chapter are on page 168.

2   The New Land

The Industrial Revolution, it is commonly believed, hit the land like some ancient barbarian conqueror, despoiling its beauty and plundering it of its riches, leaving behind some wreckage of a countryside over which future generations could lament at their leisure. Like many common beliefs it is an overdrawn picture, and this one can be corrected by any train journey of reasonable length, even through those parts—the industrial north and midlands of England, the central lowlands of Scotland, or the valleys of south Wales—that were most affected by industrial change. In all places the towns quickly give way to the countryside and on all these journeys are likely to occupy only a small part of the traveller's time.

If the extent of the devastation is commonly exaggerated, so too is the speed at which it was accomplished, for the Industrial Revolution was, in its early stages at least, a phenomenon of the countryside rather than of the towns. John Fielden was right to record that the early factories were established in 'the beautiful and romantic valleys of Derbyshire, Nottinghamshire and Lancashire', even if his claim that these became 'the dismal solitudes of torture and of many a murder' would not be universally accepted.[1] As John Jones of Bradford, Wiltshire, testified in 1803, the consequence of the introduction of machinery was that manufacturers were now on the look-out for sites to work by water; these could not be obtained in the market towns and places where the manufacture had formerly been carried on, and so in his experience the Industrial Revolution involved a movement from the towns to the countryside rather than the reverse.[2] An 1842 report of Leonard Horner, the

34

factory inspector, illustrates well the siting of some mills even at this relatively late stage, for it reads like an account of a tour of the beauty spots of the Yorkshire Dales. A round of inspection which took him to factories at Arncliffe, Grassington, Hawes, Ingleton, Kettlewell, Kirkby Malham, Linton, Pateley Bridge, Ripon, and Settle, must have been a pleasure of a toil, and no-one could today argue that these places were overwhelmed by the process of industrialisation.[3]

At the time when John Jones was giving his evidence on water-mills, the translation to steampower was, of course, well in hand elsewhere and establishing the pattern of urban industrialisation associated with the next stage of the Industrial Revolution, but that did not mean that industry was quickly to be removed from rural settings. In 1816 Dr Spiker followed a road through Derbyshire which ran parallel to the River Dove and enjoyed commanding views across the river of a scene 'full of manufactories and country houses'; the whole countryside of the area he found very picturesque. This eye for the neat antithesis, if such it was, had further opportunities to exercise itself in the neighbourhood of Halifax, where woollen and cotton factories abounded, yet the countryside around the town seemed to him 'particularly beautiful, being everywhere interspersed with handsome country houses, some of which are built even on the tops of the hills round the town'. He was delighted too by the pleasing colour of the sand-stone of which houses were built, a pleasure that is once again comprehensible to those who, after a lifetime amongst the blackened buildings, are now seeing them in their former state as a result of the modern taste for restoration and reclamation.[4]

Reactions to the new land are not easy to categorise or systematise. The foreign travellers who were merely casual visitors had usually no particular axe to grind, and their recorded comments listed personal impressions which probably tell us as much about their country of origin as of the one they believed themselves to be describing. Their criteria were either personal or external to Britain, and their comments interesting

C
35

rather than of major importance. The British travellers had their points of reference inside the country; their possible commitment to ideas and causes might have made them less than detached commentators, but at the same time it made them representative of important attitudes and traditions of thought. The Hon John Byng, for instance, though he might have been content to describe himself as a traveller, a sportsman, and a citizen—roles which scarcely compel attention for his views—emerges from his writings as a traditionalist, a paternalist and a strong opponent of those whom he believed to be using their wealth irresponsibly.[5] As such he is a characteristic figure of his age. So too were the itinerant commissioners of the 1830s and 1840s, whose descriptions frequently seem to involve flights of romantic fancy but who were professional observers concerned to draw practical conclusions from what they saw. The romantic poets and writers who concerned themselves with nature, the human condition, or an idealised past, are more important for the power of their ideas than the accuracy of their observations, whilst the comments of the political theorists and activists, like Engels or Oastler, must always be judged in the light of the purpose they were pursuing. Most observers were then either casual, insufficiently detached, or inaccurate, and it would be a mistake to expect from them a clear and coherent picture.

Perhaps it was easier for Dr Spiker as a casual visitor in the year 1815 to be charmed by the juxtaposition of industry and nature than it was for a nation twenty years later, though even in 1838 William Howitt, searching out what was left of the rural life of old England, recognised that the industrial towns of the north stood in an immediate neighbourhood of cultivated hills and beautiful, wooded valleys, from which rose up 'the tall chimneys of vast and innumerable factories': these distracted him from the beauties of the countryside and made him think rather of the horrors of the factory system and the small children employed within it.[6] His more serious mood was shared by the less romantically inclined Poor Law Commissioners of the early

1830s, engaged in their stock-taking pursuits. They reported that the country villages of Lancashire into which immigrants had flocked during the last quarter of the eighteenth century to enjoy the fleeting prosperity of weaving during its golden days, were 'more affected by commercial than by agricultural vicissitudes'.[7] The cotton trade was proving notoriously prone to periodic depression, increasing that into which the handloom weavers had been inexorably sinking since the turn of the century, and when Howitt came to describe weavers' cottages set among the hills in 1838 it was not a picture of idyllic co-existence of industry and nature. The condition of the weavers had changed, and so too had the mood. The hills had become naked, wild, and desolate, their fields sodden through want of drainage and overgrown with rushes, yet the countryside swarmed with a population of weavers, 'the people and their houses equally unparticipant of those features which delighted the poet and the painter'.[8]

And if this was what a decaying branch of the textile trade could do to one part of the countryside, the opening of a colliery had equally grim consequences for another—the area between the Weare and the Tees. Here, reported the Commissioners on Child Employment in 1842, collieries had opened up within the past ten years, requiring the creation of instant villages to serve them, a species which they illustrated with the village of Coxhoe, near Clarence Hetton colliery. This extended about a mile along both sides of the road, and there were breaks every ten or twelve houses for the streets which ran off to right and left. 'The cottages', ran the report, 'are built with stone plastered with lime, with blue slate roofs, and all appear exceedingly neat, and as like to one another as so many soldiers are like to each other.' It was a thriving and prosperous place which they described, but their description is memorable above all for the grimness and uniformity of this country village, whose houses had 'not one inch of land attached', and the speed with which it was superimposed upon the countryside.[9]

If some parts of the countryside were seen to be acquiring

industry and gaining people during these years, others were seen to be losing people and acquiring in their place either sheep or perhaps new forms of agriculture. Now no historical controversy, unless it be that concerning the condition of the factory children, has been more bitterly contested than that about the associated issues of enclosure and rural depopulation, and it could well be that on this question, as on others, historians have seen more and more clearly than contemporaries were able to see. At any rate, they have been inclined to play down the social consequences of enclosure, and to argue that it was not carried out with the inhumanity popularly associated with it, though it is not denied that specific cases of hardship resulted from it. Except where pasturing permanently replaced arable farming, enclosure might well have increased the amount of employment available as improvements were carried out, and such pressures on rural employment, agrarian distress and revolt, and migration to towns as occurred are now more likely to be seen as the consequence of population growth rather than enclosure. It is now customary to stress the limited amount of depopulation that occurred as a result of this or for any other reason. There was, in one view, no rural depopulation before 1800 and very little before 1850. That deserted villages belonged to imaginative writing rather than real life was Eden's view in 1797, and there are plenty who would be willing to echo that as a view applying equally well to the following half century.[10] Yet for all the learning and wisdom that have served to modify the old traditions, the fact remains that the old traditions developed and persisted, and evidence is not lacking that many contemporaries seemed to believe that they were witnessing a process of depopulation in some parts of the country. Whether predetermined views led them deliberately to close one eye, or they were innocently but mistakenly generalising from too limited an experience is not easy to say.

The Hon John Byng objected to enclosures in 1781 because, he said, he objected to hunters being driven off the commons and he resented 'the greedy tyrannies of the wealthy few to oppress the indigent many', which had driven away the poor from around Burford in Oxfordshire into other parts. Eleven years later, commenting on the wretched mud-walled cottages of the poor of Alderminster, who had had their 'portion of land and commonage' taken from them, he resolved that on his own estates there should be no mud cottages and that his tenants would keep their land and remain happy.[11] Byng disliked much, though not all, of what he saw of the new industrialism, and his attitudes as a land-owner were of the traditional 'paternalist' rather than modern 'improving' kind, but this hardly makes him less honest as a commentator than an enthusiast for the new trends, who might fail to see any such effects of enclosure amongst the rural poor.

William Cobbett, as always, is a slightly different proposition. In addition to being a countryman devoted to upholding the old ways of life, he was also a self-conscious publicist and polemicist, who assumed almost a natural licence to exaggerate in all that he said, which makes him an impossible source for accurate information but a quite possible one nonetheless for the detection of trends. Two examples from the *Political Register* of 1816 will illustrate his method. In April he described how London and its neighbourhood had enormously increased in buildings and population, a favourite theme for him, and contrasted this with more distant parts of the country where whole villages had become depopulated or reduced to a few miserable hovels of mud and thatch, from which he made what he regarded as the incontrovertible deduction that some parts of the country had gained in population whilst others had lost.[12] In December he made the generalisations that the lands of small farms had gone to extend the tracts of great farmers or to create parks for nabobs; labourers' cottages had become cattle sheds or fallen down, and 'many thousands of happy hamlets had been wholly deserted and destroyed', all since 1793.[13] There was a little to be said for each of the points in his argument, but in no case was he justified in carrying the argument to such extremes, exaggerations which he matched in 1824 by his claim that seven eighths at least of the country's farm houses had been destroyed, along with a similar proportion of cottages, as a result of the enclosure of wastes.[14] Pamphleteering had come to depend on caricature rather than description, and in so doing had rendered less credible the legitimate arguments that could have been put forward. These were more moderately deployed by William Howitt in 1838 when he described the hardships that befell some people who lost their common rights, the disappearance of their little flocks of sheep, their cows, their geese, or their pigs, and the hardships and sense of injustice which they experienced, rather than their wholesale disappearance which Cobbett had alleged.[15]

In Scotland too the tradition persisted and there are too many sound witnesses to permit its easy dismissal. Certainly the Highland Clearances themselves were no myth, whatever myths they served to generate. When a select committee reported on the petitions of Scottish weavers in 1811, it acknowledged that the workforce of weavers had in the early days been encouraged by the prospects in the new trade, but at the same time were obliged to leave agricultural labour because farms were being put together and cottages demolished, which had compelled people to depart for the towns.[16] Coleridge, on a Scottish tour in 1803, met an elderly widow near Fort Augustus, who recalled how recently the place had housed 'One hundred and seventy-three Christian souls, man, woman, boy, girl, babe', where now only a shepherd and his few assistants lived to tend the sheep: 'Well, but they have gone, and with them the bristled bear, and the pink haver [two cereals], and the potato plot that looked as gay as any flower-garden with its blossoms! I sometimes fancy that the very birds are gone—all but the crows and the gleads.' Nor was Coleridge able to persuade himself that 'if three were fed at Manchester instead of two at Glencoe or the Trossachs, the balance of human enjoyment was in favour of the former.'[17]

The *New Statistical Account of Scotland* in 1845 was to locate a number of ministers able to illustrate the depopulation of some

villages which they themselves served. From industrial Lanarkshire came examples such as the parish of Crawford, where the
minister attributed a decline since 1755 to the practice of
uniting small farms into one large one, a practice which he
alleged was general throughout Scotland. In the parish of
Cadder, the love of money and 'the desire to lay house to house
and field to field' were said to have turned many parts of a
once populous parish into a wilderness. The minister here made
a specific reference to Goldsmith's 'The Deserted Village', many
passages of which, he said, applied strongly and appropriately
to the parish of Cadder.[18] In the making of an industrial landscape, such declining and depopulated areas could have played
only a small part, yet the decay of the old land somehow managed to occupy a disproportionately important place in the
traditions associated with the formation of the new.

Of the characteristics associated with the new landscape,
that which stood out pre-eminently among the rest was the new
industrial town, and there is no shortage of references to the
physical impact upon their surroundings made by the new
centres of wealth and population. Many of them belonged to
Lancashire, that famous county, according to Cobbett in 1817,
'where every hamlet is a village, every village a town, and
every town a city', and Yorkshire, 'not less remarkable for the
variety of its products than that of its localities', where, according to a foreign traveller in 1825, each of its principal towns
exhibited a peculiar species of industry.[19] One witness before an
1816 enquiry remembered the time, thirty years earlier, when
a stranger approaching Manchester would see only the single
chimney of Mr Arkwright's mill.[20] Now a forest of chimneys
would greet them, such as those that first greeted Cooke Taylor
as he later stepped from the Liverpool train 'pouring forth
volumes of steam and smoke, forming an inky canopy which
seemed to embrace and involve the entire place'.[21] In Manchester, the second city of the kingdom, Southey found mul-
titudes crowded into narrow streets, houses built of brick and
blackened with smoke, and amongst them larger buildings,

ctories, as big as convents but lacking their antiquity, beauty, nd holiness.[22] This last response embodied values and emotions, expounded in his criticism of the new society and its values, quite beyond those of the impersonal and objective witness.

But before some of the grimmer aspects of industrialisation and urbanisation had become clear, some of the new towns, which later would have appalled their visitors, were not without a certain picturesque charm. Byng clearly found Rotherham a place of some fascination in 1789, a newly built and flourishing place with its cannon foundries and iron-works; there were coal-pits everywhere by the roadsides, with open shafts down which he had to peep and fling stones, at the same time wondering how the local children escaped the perils which they so menacingly posed.[23] Similarly, Gateshead, rarely to feature as a beauty spot on later occasions, appealed to Spiker in 1816, presenting him with an 'extremely picturesque' view of a town bestride a river, the south bank busy with manufacturing industry, the north full of the bustle of river vessels.[24]

As the century wore on the charm wore off, and the industrial towns made less acceptable contributions to the surrounding scenery. In the 1840s Derby poured out 'torrents of black smoke' from its chimneys, killing off all plants but deciduous shrubs in its gardens, converting its evergreens into nevergreens, and restricting their life span to a mere three or four years.[25] This problem of smoking chimneys was never satisfactorily solved, in spite of many attempts at it. The *Nottingham Journal* was happy to report, in December 1822, that the long complained of nuisance from the smoke of the steam-engine at Mr Redgate's factory had been entirely removed, thanks to the adoption of 'Mr Johnston's patent plan', but Mr Johnston's plan was evidently not widely adopted since a motion appeared before the House of Commons in 1843 demanding that factories be made to consume their own smoke.[26] In the following year, Prime Minister Peel informed the House that he understood some forty or fifty inventions existed for the abatement of this nuisance, but the nuisance remained, whether from defects in the inventions or the government's inability to enforce appropriate standards.[27] South Shields doubtless remained for a long time, as it had been in 1845, blackened with smoke and totally devoid of all trees, in small part because of its closeness to the sea 'but chiefly owing to the smoke and other exhalations from the manufactories', producing glass, alkali, soap, and ships.[28] And the physical blot on the landscape created by the towns of large industrial units was equalled by the less dramatic but still grim appearance of a town such as Wolverhampton. Here small lock-smiths, key-makers, screw-makers, and tobacco-box makers operated in their little work-shops, hidden at the backs of houses in narrow courts and unpaved yards, and evil housing and sanitation combined to produce a squalid and dirty town.[29] If modern scholars have found the new industrial towns fascinating for their contrasts rather than their uniformity of experience, and noted the opportunities for a fuller life that urban dwelling afforded, they have not been able to undermine the contemporary view that they were on the whole, noisy, dirty, unhealthy, and generally unpleasant places, despite their individual characteristics and occasional redeeming features.[30]

Awesome and grim as the new towns undoubtedly were, they were coming to be no more than the points of greatest concentration of population in larger areas which could be identified as industrial areas, possessing a landscape which was an industrial landscape. The gentle spill-over of early industry into pleasant countryside, which characterised the early stages of growth, would become more and more a memory of the past as the stamp of industry was firmly placed upon larger stretches of land. Those who attempted to convey in writing the impressions that the industrial landscape made upon them, seem to have been dominated by strong, but almost contradictory, emotions—on the one hand horror at being travellers in an alien land amongst virtual savages who might turn upon them and eat them, or at least toss them down a pit shaft or into the moving parts of one of the machines they were examining; on the other hand wonderment which turned their thrill of horror into one of delight at the miracles they were being allowed to behold, and the amazing physical images which they projected and suggested. This ambiguity is rarely absent from contemporary accounts. For all his dislike of the developments he was observing, Byng found the bridge across the Severn an object of admiration and a wonder of the modern world; the furnaces of South Yorkshire, which placed the countryside under an eternal blanket of smoke were a hateful, but an intriguing sight nonetheless as they were 'vomiting forth their amazing fires'.[31] Similarly, the writer of the *Commercial Directory* of 1814–15, found the countryside round Huddersfield bleak and barren, as the dark moorlands rose up to dominate the mills that were sited in the valleys below; the whole effect was somehow 'romantic and interesting'.[32] Even today a traveller by rail or road from Huddersfield to Manchester can hardly fail to absorb this enigmatic countryside, which alternately horrifies and stimulates through the power of its industry and its setting. Dr Spiker, travelling between Birmingham and Wolverhampton in 1816, was fascinated by the 'innumerable columns of smoke, issuing from the chimneys of the steam-engines and the furnaces, and other works, the number of which is beyond all conception'. The mind could not conceive the number of chimneys he saw; his powers of description were over-taxed by the gigantic iron bridge he saw being manufactured in Rotherham, and his whole body was unable to bear for more than a few seconds the intense heat generated as he watched molten metal flowing from the large furnaces. All was larger, or more numerous, or hotter, or more incredible than his life to that point had led him to expect.[33]

The same was true for the French visitor of 1825, who likened the underground workings of the Newcastle coal-pits to subterranean towns, which he recommended the curious to visit. Beneath the surface of the earth, some three or four hundred feet down, he found a regular network of streets which reminded him of the better parts of London, which either reflects well upon the collieries of Newcastle, or ill upon the streets of London. The whole countryside of mountains flattened into roadways, of canals linking towns with each other and the coast, 'of rivers suspended by aerial aqueducts over the most impracticable eminences; of bridges which protract their airy forms into the sea', were wonders of the new Britain which surpassed, he believed, even 'the exaggerations of eastern fairy tale'. 'When industry accelerates the march of civilisation by miracles such as these', he wrote, 'poetry may console herself for the loss of her illusions, since these new manifestations of human genius promise her a series of new images, not less sublime than those which preceded them.' The works of man were no less wonderful than the works of nature. Not all was so sublime: he had time to notice, on a more mundane level, the low huts of the working classes around Newcastle as well as the spacious mansions of the rich, although his mood was best reflected in the 'lugubrious mines' and 'the kilns, with the black vapours vomited from their fiery throats'.[34]

The last place that romantic description might be expected to be found, is in the reports of those fact-finding missionaries, who toured the country in the 1840s inspecting conditions of work, especially those of children. Yet these writings contain some of the best examples of this kind of response to the physical impact of new industry. In their first report of 1842, the Commissioners on Child Employment recorded that no-one who had made the journey between Birmingham and Wolverhampton by night, would ever forget the scene he had witnessed of blazing fires on every side from coal burning on the ground in the process of its conversion into coke, of 'blazing fields of bitumous shale and indurated clay', flames leaping from the chimneys of the great towers of the iron-furnaces, the whole scene presenting 'an impressive and even awful prospect, to which nothing usually seen by mortal eyes can be compared'. Again, this was beyond human experience; a new dimension almost had been introduced into life. Even in the daytime the picture was remarkable enough. 'Innumerable tall and hollow columns, from the summits of which issue clouds of dense smoke, with the flame and smoke from the tops of furnaces, and flames of fire on the ground, create a sensation of surprise mixed with dread.' By contrast, the most densely populated part of Staffordshire they found 'less fearful than at first anticipated'; there were good crops of grass and even of wheat 'although the heads look very black long before the time of harvest'.[35]

In the following year, the report of the Mining Commissioners on South Staffordshire described how, near Dudley, early potatoes for the London market were raised in ground heated by steam and smoke which came from an old colliery that had been on fire for many years, and which could be seen bursting through crevices in the rock by the roadside near to the town. This, together with 'the clouds of smoke from the furnaces, coke hearths, and heaps of calcining ironstone', had created an atmosphere so foul that no-one lived in the area except those who needed to do so to earn their daily bread. Depressed as this body of men must have been, they compared favourably with the next people encountered by the commissioners, who found 'the intermediate zone at the junction of the coal measures and the new red sandstone . . . occupied by a very inferior race, following the occupation of nailmaking'. This really was to the commissioners a journey among primitives in a savage and previously unknown land; the nailers, like some jungle tribe being contrasted with another, were said to be much inferior to the miners in character and to have betrayed 'a far more dangerous and savage disposition' when roused. It was with relief that the seekers after information left behind them 'the mean and wretched villages of the nailers' and the coalfields, seeing them 'replaced by wooded hills, ancient yews, and houses and cottages' of black-painted wood and whitewashed bricks, 'mantled with ivy'. Here even the trees presented a contrast with those encountered earlier. And soon they were out of the industrial area completely, among 'the venerable parish churches and the residences of nobility or gentry, surrounded with fine ancestral trees and marks of ease and agricultural life. The atmosphere has become purified from carbonic fumes; the smell of hay or turnip fields replaces the sulphurous odour and taste of coke hearths, the songs of birds greet the ear instead of the whizzing of steam, and the strokes of the flail instead of the forge hammer.'[36] The commissioners have here employed that nice line in antithesis, which was so strong in the 1840s, between town and country, industry and agriculture, and the 'two nations'—the rich and the poor. That between North and South is absent, for all the rest could be drawn from the west midland county of Staffordshire. It was the industrial areas which the commissioners had been sent out to examine, but they were happiest when they had left them behind.

Further north, similar sights had provoked similar responses. Thomas Tancred, reporting from Coatbridge in 1842, admitted quite explicitly that his powers of description were 'wholly inadequate to convey the feeling inspired by a visit to these localities'. Nevertheless he attempted to describe the physical scene before him as he climbed at night the hill on which stood the established church; 'the group of blast furnaces on all sides might be imagined to be blazing volcanoes', at most of which work was continued day and night, without intermission for seven days a week. 'By day a perpetual steam arises from the whole length of the canal, where it receives the waste water from the blast engines on both sides of it; and railroads, traversed by long trains of waggons drawn by locomotive engines intersect the country in all directions.' These were, he reported incidentally, the cause of frequent accidents, into which, under Scottish law, no inquiry was necessary—a little touch which confirmed the barbarous nature of the place in which he found himself.[37]

If this was an area which had leapt into existence over twenty years, there were others which were being transformed 'with almost fabled rapidity', and these were the new colliery districts. R. M. Franks, reporting from the Northumberland and Durham coalfields, described what happened when collieries were opened, 'how long rows of unpicturesque cottages' would be erected, at which would arrive 'waggons piled with ill-assorted furniture, the immediate importation of the very scum and offscouring of a peculiar, mischievous, and unlettered race', another addition to the savage tribes encountered earlier: and the external features of the country would immediately acquire those characteristic features recognised in all such places, 'the dense columns of rolling smoke—the endless clatter of endless strings of coal-waggons—the funereal colour imparted to the district'. All these manifestations, commented Franks, were quite enough to drive the wealthy from these places; 'the arrival of the pitmen is the signal for the departure of the gentry, and henceforward, few indeed visit that district but they who traffic with the coals or the colliers.'[38] The speed of this kind of transformation of the countryside was further illustrated by the land between the Weare and the Tees, where within ten or a dozen years an entirely new population had been produced. 'Where formerly was not a single hut of a shepherd, the lofty steam-engines of a colliery now send their volumes of smoke into the sky, and in the vicinity is a town called, as if by enchantment, into immediate existence.'[39]

Again the supernatural had intervened to create what men could now see about them, though nowhere was this sensation more keenly experienced than in those industries where dramatic landscape formed a backcloth for mighty machinery at work, provoking endless superlatives and evoking images of exotic foreign lands, of underworlds, and heavenly kingdoms. Such was Sir George Head's reaction to Low Moor iron-works, Bradford, which he visited during his tour through the manufacturing areas of England in 1835. The approach over a moor rich in iron and coal was through an area of universal combustion, which reminded him of the vicinity of a volcano crater; to see the like of this 'awful picture, produced by the combined features of fire, smoke, and ashes, an individual must bend his steps at least towards Aetna or Vesuvius.' He saw 'low-blackened buildings, containing numerous fires, for the purpose of charking the coal', and 'among the more massive piles of brickwork, broad flaring flames crawling upwards from the main furnaces exhibit an awful appearance'. The furnaces were of ten feet diameter, in design like a lime-kiln, and at the summit, 'in the midst of the eager flames, strange-looking wheels recall to the memory a whole host of mythological images—such as the instrument of torment whereon the ill-fated Ixion expiated the vengeance, not undeservedly, of ancient Jupiter.' The turning wheels pulled up iron-waggons to the furnace mouth, 'where no living power could perform the office', and there emptied their contents. It was for Head 'a noble sight to stand here and see the devastating element in such radiant glory, yet at the same time under perfect subjection'; the sounds and the visions were 'sufficient to raise, even in the apathetic mind, the sentiment of veneration'. As he gazed through furnace doors at fused metal being stirred, he perceived 'a glowing lake of fire' under the control of men who worked like the Cyclopes, and the power of the giant was conveyed too by the shears which cut iron bars one and three quarter inches thick as a ploughman might bite off the end of a carrot. And as he listened to the din of the air-blast through the main furnaces, which neither Niagara nor an Atlantic storm could rival, the sensation was so sublime that he wondered how this power might be applied to the production of music.[40] To note only the grim horrors of industrialisation and the industrial landscape would be to overlook this wide range of other emotions that the new sights were capable of arousing within their observers.

Whilst it is certainly true that many people had comments to make about the new land that industrialisation was bringing into being, a few of them enthusiastically favourable, a lot of them hostile, these observations were more in the form of *ad hoc* responses to a particular development in a particular place, rather than considered judgments or verdicts on what the entire process of industrialisation was doing to the country as a whole. If the *Manchester Mercury* should choose to go into raptures over the aqueduct that had been constructed over the Mersey at Marple—'one of the most striking objects to be seen in this or any other country . . . it unites magnificent grandeur with beneficial simplicity. . . . The wide expanse and amazing loftiness of its arches present a spectacle truly sublime'—this was a perfectly legitimate reaction to a fine human achievement, and did not necessarily carry approval for the processes of economic change that were at work, or for the other physical changes that they would effect on the landscape.[41] Similarly, when Cooke Taylor looked at certain former agricultural lands in Lancashire of no great productivity and no great worth, and saw how the advent of industry could transform land values, raising the demand for plots of land for cottages, market-gardens, and dairy-farming, and giving an impetus to farming, with 'the moor blossoming as the garden, and the desert blossoming as the rose', he was not giving his aesthetic approval to the new industrialism in all its aspects, but making a legitimate, empirical observation, albeit expressed in somewhat flowery language.[42]

And if the enthusiasts were seeing beauty where it could be seen, yet not saying that new industry was beautifying the countryside, so were the hostile critics on the whole limited and reserved in the observations which they had to make. The whole debate might on occasion seem so restrained and so peripheral in its concern as to have a strong air of unreality about it, being far removed from the passionate arguments that would grow up later in the century. The *Manchester Guardian*, for example, in the 1820s, was concerned that the labouring classes should be confined to factories six days a week, and urged that Sunday should be a day of relaxation for breathing the pure air and enjoying the scenery of the countryside: but this did not lead the editor towards an attack upon the destructive atmosphere of Manchester, which Robert Owen condemned as unfit for humans to breathe, but towards a campaign for the preservation of ancient footpaths, a matter of some importance but hardly the most central and pressing issue of the day.[43] With similar mildness and unconscious irony, the paper offered gentle approval for the new Manchester, in 1823, by congratulating the townsfolk on the erection of 'two handsome and substantial buildings'—two new shops in Market Street![44] The 'footpaths' theme was taken up by the Factory Commissioners, in 1833, who regretted the absence of gardens, parks, and walls at Manchester, as a result of which factory workers were not able 'to taste the breath of nature or look on its verdure'. But this was neither a fundamental analysis of what was wrong with Manchester, nor a generalisation on the effects of the factory system.[45] When Lord Ellenbrough opposed the repeal of the Spitalfields Acts in 1823 because 'he did not wish to see another Manchester growing up near the metropolis', he probably meant just that, and his words do not contain any generalised response or attitude.[46] Indeed, parliamentary debates through half a century of industrialisation are virtually devoid of comment on the aesthetic aspects of industrialism, which suggests either a legislature of philistines or else that this is too early a point in time to find anything beyond individual responses to individual experiences.

This proposition is well illustrated by the responses of landowners to the advent of industry on their own estates and in the vicinity of their homes. They might well have objections to specific schemes, such as a projected railway across their lands, because it would destroy their amenities or those of their tenants or pose a threat to the farming of their tenants. Similarly, the development of coalmines and urban expansion might both threaten the character of their estates and precipitate the erection of buildings within sight of a hall which had previously stood undisturbed. In order to frustrate land developers in 1806, one of Lord Dartmouth's agents was instructed to bid for land near Sandwell Hall, close to West Bromwich, to spare the landowner this experience. Similarly, in 1836, Ralph Sneyd was prepared to buy land to keep himself away from 'that foul smithy Newcastle' (-under-Lyme). Yet Dartmouth was an enthusiastic industrialist, as was Sneyd's father, and opposition to railways could well have derived from investment in canals, and hostility towards mines close at hand did not necessarily imply hostility to mines at a distance.[47] The individual balanced the value of the additional income against the blemish to the landscape where his own landed property was concerned; where his economic investments offended only the aesthetic sensibilities of others, he was not inhibited by any delicacy of taste which threatened to turn a personal disinclination into a matter of general principle.

Statements of general principle were in fact few and far between. Byng, even in the eighteenth century, had expressed his dislike of 'great, black manufacturing towns', and lamented that Arkwright and his emulators had 'crept into every pastoral vale' and 'destroyed the course and beauty of nature'.[48] He might have been worried specifically about Arkwright and his cotton mills, but this statement came very close to being a generalised response to a whole process of industrialisation. Another critic who generalised was Robert Southey. Undoubtedly Manchester held a particular horror for him, but his comments applied to the system as a whole, that everything connected with manufactures revealed features of 'unqualified deformity', such as the rows of cottages erected to house the new industrial workforce.[49] This is a foretaste of the major critics of industrialism, John Ruskin and William Morris, who would take up this and other points in the third and fourth quarters of the nineteenth century. And perhaps it required D. H. Lawrence in the twentieth century to stand right back from the whole process of industrialisation and assess what impact it had made on the countryside which experienced the Industrial Revolution of the late eighteenth and early nineteenth centuries. On this issue, as on so many others, contemporaries were able to offer little more than fairly superficial and personal responses to their own experiences, and were denied the perspective necessary for penetrating analysis.

Notes to this chapter are on page 171.

3 The New Society

If the physical impact of the Industrial Revolution upon the land is something that could not be fully appreciated instantly, how much more true this is of its impact upon society. The fact that people are still arguing bitterly and at great length about the social consequences of industrialisation, suggests that contemporary comment on this subject might supply only the merest clues to the true nature of the picture that will eventually emerge. And yet it could be argued that most of the pieces had already been identified before the middle of the nineteenth century and that their arrangement was then, as it remains now, as much a matter of taste as of objective observation.

The new towns were less important as blots on the physical landscape than as places where people lived, and the new society that occupied the new land was increasingly an urban society. For a long time the shortcomings of the new towns seemed to outnumber the virtues they displayed and the advantages they offered, and it can safely be said that their critics were much more in evidence than their defenders during the first half of the nineteenth century. A majority would doubtless have echoed Sir Frederick Eden's value judgment of 1797 that agricultural life was better than manufacturing life.[1] Country living was thought better than town living without there being any obvious need to lay down precise criteria. Such reputation as towns had for vice and depravity was only confirmed and strengthened during the early decades of industrialisation, and the feeling persisted that towns were somehow a perversion of nature and not the intended habitat of man on earth. This was partly because towns were built for work and not for living, a

53

distinction which men were for the first time coming to draw. Their most important buildings were their factories and workshops, and their houses serviced the workforce, being constructed for the functions of eating and sleeping, not for the pleasures of living. Men were brought to towns purely by the desire for gain, according to Disraeli; as a result they lived there not in a state of co-operation but in one of isolation.[2] The same feeling was expressed by a Scottish minister in the 1840s who complained that 'There is no community . . . there is aggregation . . . modern society acknowledges no neighbours.'[3] Wordsworth believed that this 'unnatural clustering' weakened men's bodies, inflamed their passions, undermined their moral affections, and destroyed their imagination.[4] George Eliot was similarly impressed by the 'unnatural' quality of life in the industrial towns, the deformity of the miner, the pallor of the weaver, the neglected child of the overworked mother, all of them contrary to nature's intention.[5] And Elizabeth Gaskell, in *North and South*, commented on the 'depression and worry of spirits'—suffered by the confined townsman who spent little of his time out of doors—which was induced in part by the social insecurity said to beat at the heart of the industrial, and consequently of the urban, system.[6]

Some of these opinions would still meet with widespread approval, though it is now clear that contemporary observers passed some very superficial judgments on many aspects of urban life, in particular when they bleakly assumed the town-worker to be living and working in a state of isolation, without community and with no co-operation from his fellows. Even the factory was capable of forming new loyalties and bonds of identity amongst its workmen, whilst local communities within towns might provide a framework for social life that did much to counteract the dehumanising tendencies so frequently noted. Above all, social existence was determined by the continued overwhelming importance of kinship links within the new industrial communities. Although urban life and factory employment offered opportunities for earlier economic independence for young people, a factor supporting the contemporary view of the break-up of the family, links of kinship remained of central importance, especially during times of crisis.[7]

If towns were thought to be unnatural growths, it is not surprising that they should have been recognised as places of disturbance and trouble. 'It is in trading towns only', recorded Byng in 1792, 'where rioting and discords begin', and if rioting was at this period sufficiently widespread throughout the countryside as a whole to make this observation unfair, the industrial and political upheavals of 1812 and the post-war years confirmed the general belief that manufacturing areas were places of trouble.[8] 'The disturbed districts' was virtually a synonym for the manufacturing districts, and the House of Commons was informed in 1819 that this was because they experienced the greatest distress and misery.[9] An alternative explanation for their notoriety was given by the Earl of Darnley in 1815, when he argued that the manufacturing population crowded into the great towns was better able to draw organised attention to itself.[10]

Others saw that the problem lay partly in the breakdown of the machinery of law and order, that as the towns grew and became more unattractive, the magisterial class retreated into the country at a time when its services were most needed in the urban centres, which in most cases were unincorporated areas.[11] In their absence, there grew up that fabled race of urban trouble-makers who supplied, for instance, the leaders of the machine-breakers in Charlotte Brontë's *Shirley*; they were 'emissaries from the towns', not genuine operatives with genuine grievances, but 'bankrupts, men in debt and drink'.[12] Their criminal propensities were notorious, though more magnified than quantified. The Sheriff of Lanarkshire, A. Allison, testified in 1838 that from his own observation, unfortunately not backed up by relevant figures, over eighteen years, there was 'six times as much crime in the manufacturing districts, in proportion, as in the rural, I mean actually committed; taking in view the difference in the strictness of the police, probably it is

55

ten times greater'.[13] When the *Manchester Guardian* attempted to explain this kind of situation in July 1838, it accepted the urban reputation as justified, and explained high crime rates in terms of the greater opportunities open to criminals in towns and the passivity of a homogeneous agricultural society in the villages.[14]

The absence of statistics for crimes committed in the first half of the nineteenth century makes modern commentators more reluctant to make extravagant contrasts between the new industrial towns and other places, but they would probably agree that a young, unsettled population, poor physical environment, and inadequate social facilities all helped to push up crime figures in the new towns.[15]

Accompanying urban crime was that favourite target of the socially respectable, working-class vice, for vice was a purely proletarian prerogative at this time and had still to lose its social exclusiveness, which went with a more egalitarian society of later times. Where, asked William Howitt, was there such vice and misery as in the manufacturing towns, and the universally agreed answer was that they had no rivals in this respect.[16] But if the early Victorians were more obsessed with vice than people today, they had much less sophisticated ideas about its possibilities, and their main preoccupations were the intemperance and lax sexual behaviour of the working classes. Populous districts always meant a deterioration in moral conditions, according to Peter Gaskell; Manchester alone had almost a thousand inns, and in towns, according to an enquiry into the working of the new Poor Law, people were more likely to indulge each other, spend more, and be tempted to intemperance.[17] A correspondent for the *Manchester Mercury* of February 1816, worried that 'every night furnishes fresh proof of the depravity which fills our streets', no doubt deplored drunkenness and prostitution, for Manchester 'like all large manufacturing towns', according to the *Guardian*, was 'fraught with more than average danger to the morals of the young'.[18] These problems should not, of course, be underestimated, but few contemporaries had the insight to realise that they were symptoms and consequences of what was wrong with the new industrial towns, rather than fundamental causes.

It might be assumed from the unflattering references made to towns at the end of the eighteenth or in the early years of the nineteenth century, that there was an early awareness of an urban social problem that required action, but this again would be to attribute to contemporaries a clarity of view which they did not possess. An isolated number of the *Manchester Mercury* complained, in December 1805, of a specific nuisance, namely the slaughter of pigs in narrow streets and the noxious smells arising from the fumes of boiled pork.[19] An isolated number of the *Nottingham Review* complained in August, 1811, that the River Leen, the source of part of the town's water supply, was being used as a dump for refuse and was therefore a threat to the town's health.[20] But these examples did not add up to any general awareness that a new kind of urban society was coming into existence, creating or intensifying a whole range of problems that could not be ignored for much longer. In 1827, an expert on insurance testified before an enquiry into friendly societies, that there was no objection to applying common tables to town and country, though an opinion was offered, as an opinion, that mortality rates were probably higher amongst the working classes than in other social groups.[21] It was, above all, the cholera epidemic of 1832 which compelled attention to be given to the towns, and prompted the first careful investigations of urban society and diagnoses of its problems. Even then the concern manifested itself in a slightly peripheral campaign for the preservation of ancient footpaths in and around the new towns, and as late as 1844 the town commissioners were notified that only recently had local authorities and principal inhabitants become aware of the extent of mortality in Liverpool, and that the 'wealthy and intelligent' were 'for the most part becoming alive to the condition of the poorer inhabitants'.[22] Still, however slow the message was in being spread, however whimsical a solution some people had to offer, and however

57

y the authorities might be in responding, Dr Kay's enquiry ɔ *The Moral and Physical Condition of the Working Classes* of ̶ ̶ ̶nchester, published in 1832, was an historic pronunciation on a problem recognised as existing on a grand scale.

It has now become such a commonplace reminder from historians not to confuse industrialisation with urbanisation, and they are so anxious to be fair to all parties involved, that the causal link between the two is in danger of being under-stressed. Towns grew and became what they were in large measure because of the growth of industry within them, and it is an artificial distinction which dwells on the horrors of the new towns and at the same time extols the virtues of the new industries. This distinction has a long and illustrious parentage, even though the writings of its creators can now be seen to contain a large element of propaganda, presenting only one side of a hotly contested debate. The other side was most simply and dramatically put by William Cobbett. He had written in 1811 of the misery in all its horrors—hunger, filth, and disease—that was to be encountered in the dwellings of manufacturing towns, and he had asked how many travellers had passed through the manufacturing towns without being waylaid at the entrance and exit by swarms of half-naked children trying to beg enough to buy an ounce of bread.[23] That had been during the severe commercial depression of 1811–12, during which Luddism had occurred. In 1824, he wrote at great length a general reflection on the 'Growth of Manufactures', in which he attacked the evils of factory labour, the air-pollution of the manufacturing town, the 'thousands upon thousands . . . slaughtered by consumption before they arrive at the age of sixteen', and described Manchester as 'that blood-stained town'. For Cobbett, industrialisation was clearly and incontrovertibly the fundamental cause of the horrors of the manufacturing towns.[24]

A little book of 1832, written by Dr Kay, an evangelical churchman who was not hostile to industrialisation as such and believed that its attendant ills could be cured by physical and moral reform, took a totally different view of the urban problem; the evils of Manchester, 'so far from being the necessary consequences of the manufacturing system, have a remote and accidental origin and might by judicious management be entirely removed'.[25] The 'judicious management' would involve cleaning up the streets, attending to working-class housing conditions, establishing schools, and repealing the Corn Laws: above all it required that the working classes should improve themselves, stop their drinking and other bad habits, and start behaving properly in the better surroundings that enlightened men such as Dr Kay would arrange for them. Industrialisation was not guilty. The blame lay elsewhere than with the manufacturers and their creations, and this theme was rapidly developed. It was the failings of the towns, not the conditions of the factories, said Leeds flax-spinner John Marshall, in 1833, which caused the miseries of the poor in Leeds, where benevolent doctors exposed the horrors of working-class housing.[26] Manchester's suffering arose from purely physical causes, which could be eliminated by resolute action, and had nothing to do with manufacturers, argued Cooke Taylor, who went on to attack the town for not making its gardens accessible to the poor.[27] The housing was to blame, said Nassau Senior, not the factories.[28] And so there developed, in the 1830s and 1840s, concern for public health, a desire to promote better housing and sanitary reform, and a concern that education should inculcate the right attitudes, which, it was believed, would tackle the problem exposed by the cholera epidemic and subsequent investigations. This was the alternative diagnosis of the nature of the urban problem, and rival interpretations of its nature were, of course, to produce rival approaches towards its solution when the legislators began to act.

This split marks a fairly advanced stage in contemporary awareness of the course of industrial change, and a beginning of more mature analysis. Prior to this most people had, in their state of innocence and unsophistication, been more conscious of the new element of instability that industrialisation had brought into society. As Mr Balwhidder surveyed the new economic activity that the cotton mill had brought to his Scottish parish in 1807, he reflected that commercial prosperity 'flush as it might be, was but a perishable commodity', whilst a foreign tourist, surveying England's external signs of prosperity in 1825, philosophised that the country would never appear more flourishing than on 'the evening before the inevitable deluge occurs to swallow it up for ever'.[29] The feeling was strong and fairly general that the new prosperity was possibly but a transitory thing, that Britain might be experiencing a temporary boost through her manufacturing industries, but other countries might supplant her in this area. The land would always remain, but industries rose and fell. The manufacturers themselves were in part responsible for this kind of belief, as they self-pityingly exaggerated the hardships under which they operated—taxation and foreign competition—and stressed the precarious nature of the supposedly modest prosperity which they were enjoying.

And if industrial prosperity had an uncertain future, it most certainly appeared to have an unstable and fluctuating present course, which carried its workforce between peaks of relative prosperity and depths of poverty and depression. From the ranks of the hostile poets, Coleridge commented on the fluctuations in wages which subjected 'the mechanics and lower ranks of our cities and towns' to alternate privation and excess, as a result of which they became improvident, discontented, and given to 'factious confederacy'.[30] Southey said almost the same thing, believing the working classes to be improvident when in receipt of good wages, and feeling themselves injured when in receipt of bad.[31] These fluctuations were believed to be in the nature of things. 'Commercial and manufacturing communities', admitted the *Manchester Guardian* from the heart of the principal one, 'are peculiarly subject to vicissitudes.'[32] In consequence, alternate prosperity and distress would always be unavoidable. Again, in June 1831, it maintained that 'occasional periods of embarrassment and distress' were 'apparently inseparable from a great commercial community'.[33] Or again, in October 1835, it reported a fall in emigration but predicted its revival once the labour market was again overstocked and distress had returned.[34] What the country was experiencing was cyclical depression, even if it had not formalised the concept, and each bout was brought to the attention of Parliament by petitions and speeches, which served to give the uninformed members of Parliament the impression that manufacturing was synonymous with distress and depression rather than with prosperity. Distress arising from commercial depression remained a convenient argument for the free traders until the repeal of the Corn Laws in 1846, even though it had by this time become equally convenient to blame working-class distress upon working-class moral failings or the jerry-builders of towns. And the proneness of early nineteenth-century workers to cyclical depression has continued to feature prominently in the modern debate on the standard of living.

Though the apportioning of blame was usually an exercise of prejudice rather than judicial impartiality, the still small voice of humanity often managed to make itself heard. Even an assistant Poor Law Commissioner reported from Cheshire that there were people who, by the utmost efforts of industry and frugality, were still not able to earn enough to support themselves; it was, he said, in no-one's interest to deny that many such people existed in manufacturing towns, and it would be wrong to withhold charity from them.[35] In 1838 a select committee on the working of the new Poor Law, recognised that in large manufacturing communities, great numbers became unemployed for long periods and needed to be given outdoor relief, which some assistant commissioners had already sanctioned. This view undermined the opinion of assistant commissioner Richard Hall, that the 1834 Act should be just as applicable to manufacturing as to agricultural areas.[36] The manufacturing industries did have their calamities, and some ministers reported in the *New Statistical Account* in the 1840s that manufacturing prosperity was accompanied by an increase in

61

pauperism. In both Paisley and Arbroath, for instance, hardship was reported through unemployment arising out of bankruptcies amongst industrialists.[37]

The growth of industry had many social consequences but none more hotly debated than that new way of life for working men, the factory system. It has already been seen that factories were unpopular during their early years, and the reasons for this were many and widely expressed. The workmen themselves often declared a preference for working at home—the life they were accustomed to—a preference illustrated in 1803 by a witness's statement that he would rather work at half rate at home than be employed in a factory.[38] The new labour also robbed the worker of his master status; he lost his valued independence, real or to some extent imagined, and became merely one of a host of undifferentiated equals. The early factories had similar connotations to that other public institution, the workhouse, and a real fear and hatred of them emerges sharply from the testimony of many witnesses at the early enquiries on the manufacturing trades. There was a general belief too that factories were corrupting for their employees, and encouraged an 'abandonment to vice' as Byng put it in 1792.[39] Some men went to factories for the specific purpose of acquiring loose habits, testified one witness in 1806.[40] More general was the belief that they were a threat to the morals of rising generations, and as late as 1841, the argument was still being advanced that they were a bad influence on young unmarried men and women.[41] They were believed to be a gathering place for the socially undesirable, not surprisingly in view of the nature of the early workforce—'transient, marginal, and deviant,' according to one modern authority—and were often considered a great nuisance to the area where they were situated.[42] The Manchester Health Board believed them responsible for the outbreaks of fever and the filling of the local hospitals in 1796, and it was 'well-known', according to the Marquis of Landsdowne in 1815, that the crowding together of large bodies of people was unfavourable to health.[43] This remained 'well-known' to many people, though there were others equally prepared to argue a contrary case. And if this remained a matter of argument, there could be no disputing Gaskell's claim in 1836 that families were no longer labouring in common and that the ties of home were being disrupted by factory work.[44]

All these claims and arguments, justified or otherwise, led to the most extreme contemporary judgments being passed upon the factory system and its role within society. Lord Ashley, the Tory reformer, condemned 'the most abominable system that ever prevailed in any civilised society'; a correspondent of the *Leeds Mercury* believed that nothing had done more to injure health, contaminate workers, perpetuate ignorance, and foster crime; and Cobbett, never to be outdone on any issue, talked of the great injury done to the country by factories 'at Manchester, Leeds, Glasgow, Paisley, and other Hell-Holes of 84 degrees of heat' where 'misery walks abroad in skin, bone, and nakedness' among 'slaves in manufactories' infinitely worse off than slaves in the West Indies.[45-7]

In this way the case against factories was reduced to a polemic, perhaps a necessary part of all great protest campaigns, but the extreme language of someone like Cobbett should not be allowed to obscure the wider concern at the social consequences of factory labour. The break-up of the family unit, more apparent than real, which for Gaskell was fundamental, was commented on too by Richard Oastler. He also observed the new rigour and regulation in mill-labour, where the boss would lay down the law, and workers would find themselves virtually removed from the protection of the law of the land operating beyond the factory walls.[48] Having escaped from feudalism, they were once again being treated as chattels, not as human beings, argued Engels, and the slavery theme was strong; the men were slaves of their masters or alternatively, 'slaves of the steam-engine'; their employment in such a capacity dehumanised their employers as much as the workers themselves, argued Southey, thereby anticipating Carlyle's better-known aphorism that 'men are grown mechanical in head and in

63

art'.[49] Men were wasting their vital energies in vain competition against the driving of wheels and the urging of steam-engines, wrote Howitt, and the technological changes which had occasioned such huge productivity, had, according to Robert Owen, brought nothing but misery and degradation to labour; the condition of society had deteriorated, not improved, as a result of new organisations and new methods.[50] No longer were working men valued as people. 'The poor English creatures who are compelled to work on the wool of this accursed weed, which has done so much mischief to England', were the tools of their employers, who incurred no obligations that were not covered by the weekly wage; for cash payment, in Carlyle's memorable expression, had become the 'sole nexus' of the relationship between the new employer and his wage labourers.[51] This was the new way of life that the factory embodied.

Of course, it did not appear like this to everyone. Sir George Phillips informed the House of Commons in 1830 that those people who were employed in factories were better off than those who were not, and that they were also better off than the factory workers of forty years previously.[52] Sir George Head, on his tour of the manufacturing districts in 1835, experienced 'happy release' from his previous opinions; the factory workers he saw seemed happy beings, their work-places lofty and well-ventilated, and their lot one that compared most favourably with that of the domestic weaver.[53] Leonard Horner, the factory inspector, produced enthusiastic descriptions of the good appearance and health of the workforce in 1837, and a further official report of 1842 stressed the advantages the factory workers were enjoying in terms of being more intelligent, better informed, and more involved citizens than they had ever been as domestic workers.[54] Even their long hours of work were not excessive, argued the flax-spinner John Marshall of Leeds; the workers' problems arose not from overwork but want of moral and religious education, the existence of beer-shops, and the absence of a police-force.[55] In other words, urbanisation, not industrialisation, had created the problems. On the relative

64

contributions made by them to the workers' dilemma, it is not possible to offer any final verdict, though the growth of a factory movement and the willingness of the government to act on factory reform in 1833, suggest a general acceptance that some sort of social problem was recognised to exist and to require action. The factory was necessary, Oastler accepted, but not necessarily an evil.[56] The factory system could not be abandoned, argued the *Leeds Mercury* in October 1830; it should therefore be reformed, it conceded, and there were few not prepared to go as far as this.[57]

Where the modern debate has probably cast most new light on this old controversy has been in the fuller understanding now possible of the technical problems of the early factory owners and managers, who strove to create a disciplined workforce out of unpromising material. But the more tolerant understanding now shown has not robbed the factories of their emotive charge.[58]

The reason why government intervention was tolerated, was not so much the effect of the factory system on the adult labour force as the outcry that arose over the whole issue of child labour. Indeed, the outcry has continued to reverberate through academic corridors over a matter which, above all others, is popularly identified with the process of industrialisation. According to an early historian of the factory movement, S. H. Kydd, in 1857, the parliamentary records of more than half a century testify to the importance of the factory question in the eyes of the legislature, but a modern reader would probably be more impressed by the sparseness of the references to this issue before 1830.[59] Pitt had given his blessing to child labour in 1796 when he reported that experience had already shown how much could be done by the industry of children and how advantageous it was to employ them early, and few members of Parliament quarrelled with this view, if they thought about the matter at all.[60] Very occasionally, there was a sign that the odd member was aware of how the new cotton industry was being manned and that this raised questions about which Parliament ought to be concerned. If Mr Wilbraham Bootle or Sir Robert Peel raised the matter of the pauper apprentices, and tried to limit their numbers or the distances they were removed from their own areas or make some other regulation for their supervision, he would be listened to with sympathy if not enthusiasm. When, however, Peel attempted to extend parliamentary concern to young children in general, in 1815, he found members either unwilling, like Kirkman Finlay the Glasgow cotton manufacturer, to worry about 'free labour', or unable to appreciate the very existence of a child employment problem beyond that of the pauper apprentices.[61] In 1818, Sir John Jackson used the evocative, if provocative, comparison with West Indian slaves to enquire why members should not be prepared to do something for their 'fellow-subjects' at home, and Peel argued that a ten-fold increase in child employment, compared with 1802, demanded a measure of interference, which first came, on a very restricted basis, in 1819.[62] Later leaders of the movement for factory reform, such as Oastler and Shaftesbury, doubtless believed that a full and public exposure of the evils they denounced would go a long way to ensuring their removal. But the capacity of a society to keep from itself information which it prefers not to have is very considerable.

The occasional references in Parliament are paralleled by occasional references in the press or in other publications, which hint at a vague unease which was never allowed to develop into a general awareness that might provoke political protest. As early as 1797, Eden had posed the classic moral dilemma of the new factory industries, whether any manufacture should be tolerated which could only be successfully conducted by the use of intolerable means, in this case the 'ransacking of cottages and houses for poor children', but the moral issue was dodged in this and in later forms.[63] In December 1805, the *Nottingham Journal* referred somewhat vaguely to the great numbers of children labouring in manufacturing towns to procure the means of subsistence, and conveyed a general impression that this was an unhappy state of affairs but did not spell out the details.[64] Similarly, the *Manchester Mercury*, in September 1810, reporting local appointments of mill-visitors, suggested that if Peel's Act of 1802 to regulate the treatment of apprentices were better known and observed, their situation would be much more comfortable; it made no attempt to describe their existing condition.[65] The hints were dropped for those who chose to take them. One who later confessed himself totally unaware of what had been going on around him was Richard Oastler, whose awakening took place on a visit to the Bradford mills of John Wood in 1830, though he had for years been accustomed to seeing the lights of working factories without questioning what went on within them.[66]

What exactly did go on within them has never been successfully resolved. According to John Fielden, himself a factory owner, children were 'flogged, fettered, and tortured in the most exquisite refinement of cruelty' in the mills of the late eighteenth century, though few went so far in suggesting a deliberate and systematised cruelty.[67] It was more common to list the deprivation that resulted from factory employment. Southey, for instance, lamented that the factory children were deprived of fresh air by day and natural sleep by night, that they lost both enjoyment and instruction, as a result of which the girls knew nothing of domestic work, how to mend a stocking or boil a potato.[68] Shelley, similarly, saw children being turned into lifeless, bloodless machines at an age when they should have been at play, whilst Howitt found them 'stunted and blighted in body and mind' as a result of the 'noise, labour, and foul atmosphere of the cotton purgatories'.[69] Opponents of child-employment agreed, more perhaps as a matter of faith than of demonstrable fact, with the findings of the factory inspector Powers, a man of more practical experience than the poets, that at Bradford a 'large mass of deformity' had been produced by the factory system. This was just as strongly denied, again as a matter of faith, by their opponents in debate.[70]

E

Not surprisingly, the argument that probably clinched the case for intervention was the one that factory children were being denied opportunities for education and, thereby, for moral improvement, a consideration to melt all but the hardest nineteenth-century hearts. As early as 1816, Robert Owen had revealed to the Child Employment Commissioners the highly suggestive information that Manchester children who attended school stayed there on average for four months, whereas Newcastle children, with no factories to draw them away, stayed at school for an average of four years each.[71] The Factory Commissioners of 1833, justified their recommendations in large measure by the absence of educational opportunity, which they sought to remedy through the schooling clause of the 1833 Factory Act.

But just as Eden had raised a general moral question in 1797, so did William Cobbett imply moral censure in his bitterly ironic discovery in 1833 that national wealth, power, and security were all dependent on the labour of 300,000 little girls in Lancashire.[72] It might have appeared to Andrew Ure in 1835 that 'the work of these lively elves seemed to resemble a sport'; the Leeds Mercury, not the most objective of commentators, might have protested that no children suffered injury through working a mere eleven hours per day; and a similarly committed Leeds factory owner might have argued that if the men would curb their drinking they could keep more of their children at home; but attempts to shift the blame for an evil, deny that an evil existed, or argue that an evil was a blessing, all left Cobbett with substantial grounds for criticising the new society—if the employment of children was an indispensable institution of this new society there was something fundamentally rotten about it.[73] The responses of historians to Cobbett's proposition remain amongst the most intimate and revealing of all self-disclosures, and their attitudes are basically of two kinds—that of persisting moral outrage at the iniquity of the practice, and that of colder rationality which affects to explain and understand but not to judge.[74]

68

New institutions, the towns and their factories, were producing, as the Elder Peel put it, 'an additional race of men, and the character and quality of its people constitute a principal test of the new society'.[75] In Shelley's still pessimistic view, the majority of the people of England were, in 1819, 'destitute and miserable, ill-clothed, ill-fed, and ill-educated', and if this opinion would nowadays seem to require various qualifications, it did in its own day broadly represent a very common view of the consequences of economic change.[76] Physically, the manufacturing population of the towns must have been quite daunting in their appearance, however this is explained. A certain Miss Spencer, travelling north, visited Manchester in 1807 and found on her approach to the manufacturing districts that the apparel of the women she saw was scarcely decent, and that all their children were without shoes and stockings. In Manchester itself people had a 'rude and uncultivated appearance' and 'a demeanour remarkably forbidding'; she had heard this to be so in manufacturing towns but this was her first opportunity of observing the phenomenon for herself.[77] Most travellers to Manchester, according to Dr Hawkins in his testimony of 1833, were 'struck by the lowness of stature, the leanness, and the paleness which present themselves so commonly to the eye . . . above all among the factory classes'; he himself had been in no European town 'in which degeneracy of form and colour from the national standard has been so obvious'. The pallor of the factory workers was almost proverbial, so much so in fact, that a factory champion like Cooke Taylor accepted it as a fact, and simply denied that it was indicative of bad health.[78] Dr Hawkins accepted the bad health, but blamed 'local defects' as well as factories.

An interesting personal recollection was given to the Factory Commissioners in 1833 by Titus Rowbotham, a 51-year-old worker from Macclesfield, who had moved to Manchester in 1801. He and his contemporaries, he said, had been brought up to out-door employments before going into factories; their children, kept in factories, became feebler in frame than their parents, and their children in turn were feebler still. In recalling the earlier generations he testified:

The impressions of those days are very vivid; I can call their images, though they have been long in their coffins: I must see the grandchildren of those I saw when I first came to Manchester, for I see my own grandchildren, and I see now men who are of my own age, and even younger than me, but who have passed their lives in mule-spinning. Their intellect has shrunk up and become dry like a tree, and they have become children again, and they are not the same men that I remember them to have been. I know many such instances.[79]

Such testimony is a personal and subjective observation of one man, but it carries conviction and must at least be considered alongside the less sympathetic comments of Dr Kay, who thought that the physical condition of the working classes could be blamed in large part upon their disgusting eating habits, the content of their diet and the way in which it was consumed.[80] But as with all generalisations at this time, those that emphasised the deplorable physical condition of the manufacturing population cannot be cited without reference to the contrary viewpoint, not so commonly found, but strongly argued nonetheless by those like the factory inspector Leonard Horner, who went out of his way in 1837 to emphasise the 'virtue, intelligence, comfort, and happiness' of 'well-fed, well-clothed, healthy and cheerful-looking' factory employees.[81]

Contemporaries found it impossible to agree on the physical condition of the new manufacturing classes, and medical authorities only contradicted each other, from ignorance as much as from partiality. The deficiencies in their knowledge and the quality of their observation might suitably be illustrated from some of their comments on coalmining as an industrial occupation. The unhealthiness of this activity might not be expected to have been so contentious a subject as that of factory employment, and there was indeed a fair measure of unanimity, though of a surprising kind. Although the Hon John Byng had believed that 1/4d (6½p) per day was not excessive pay for colliers, when it frequently happened that many were burnt to death by foul air catching fire, the view persisted that coal-mining was rather a healthy occupation with many advantages.[82] The miners, observed one visitor in 1825, were men of regular health, since they were preserved from the 'vicissitudes of the seasons' and received air in 'sufficient doses' and 'frequently renewed'.[83] Official approval was given to this view by the Mining Commissioners in 1842, who reported that the air was evidently good for people since it gave them an appetite, as a result of which persons previously lean became fat, apparently a sure sign of good health. Colliers as a whole were a healthy race, and in so far as they suffered from disease this resulted from drinking strong beer, a moral failing which bedevilled their class as a whole. Admittedly their work was laborious and exhausting, consequently, though they were healthy beings, they were not long-lived.[84] The shortness of the miner's life was evidently thought to be compensated for by the superb physical condition which characterised those few years he was able to enjoy below ground, stuffing himself with food and drink and protected from the rain and the cold. Some of these arguments were still being advanced as late as 1892 before the Royal Commission on Labour, when evidence was given on the healthy environment in which coalminers worked.[85]

However robust or debilitated the physique of the urban factory worker, it was by common consent inferior to that of the agricultural labourer, though a naval medical officer, R. M. Martin, testified in 1834 that on his return home after ten years abroad, nothing struck him with more horror than the deterioration in the physical appearance of the population, to be observed in the agricultural as well as in the manufacturing communities.[86] In general, however, it was the urban workers who were the more alarming spectacle—Commissioner R. D. Grainger reported from Birmingham in 1842 that the physical condition of the population there, as in all other manufacturing towns, was 'decidedly inferior to that of the agricultural districts'.[87] There was little disputing Cobbett's claim that a family reared by the side of a common was 'clearly distinguishable from a family bred in the pestiferous stench of the dark alleys of a town', and the difference was thought to be one of character as well as of physical appearance.[88] Lancashire itself illustrated to William Howitt 'the vast difference between the character and habits of the working class and the character and habits of the pastoral and agricultural districts.'[89] The latter were superior in condition and manners, possessing still that 'wonted simplicity of our country ways', whose loss the Rev Balwhidder had lamented in 1788 when his factory-working parishioners began reading newspapers, debating the affairs of France, and acquiring unsettling notions about religion.[90] The idealisation of pre-industrial man constantly accompanied laments over the members of the new society, and if poor countryfolk were not the morally superior beings that they were frequently believed to be, they had, as Chadwick effectively demonstrated in 1842, a dramatically higher expectancy than their urban counterparts, amongst whom disease and high mortality rates could be clearly attributed to their insanitary existence.[91]

But the really disturbing thing about the industrial working classes was not their uncouth appearance or alarming physical condition but their moral degeneracy, their propensity to vice which was giving the towns such an evil reputation and creating such despair amongst touring commissioners of the 1830s and 1840s wherever they found working men congregated in large numbers. The great theme of the 1840s, exemplified by the reports of the Mining Commissioners, was 'material unaccompanied by moral progress', or, in the language of the *New Statistical Account of Scotland*, 'material growth accompanied by moral and religious decline'.[92] But for the neglect of 'moral discipline', reported Dr Baker from Leeds in 1842, mills, manufactories, and workshops might have been blessings wherever they were erected.[93] With the neglect of moral welfare, the state of working-class morals and manners was 'terrible', and far worse than the casual observer assumed, wrote Howitt in 1838, whilst Dr Gaskell asserted with confidence that 'the domestic artisan as a moral and social being was infinitely superior to the manufacturer of a later date.'[94] The language of these denunciations is often vague and ambiguous. Cobbett, usually the most forthright of men, in attacking 'hotbeds of vice and corruption', reminded his readers that all congregation of people together in great numbers was known to be 'productive of impurity of thought and manners', which he illustrated by his own particular favourite corruption, tea-drinking, a more costly habit than those associated with the consumption of malt.[95] Others were less quirkish and more systematic in their analysis of the working-class predicament, like the Staffordshire clergyman in 1842, who declared his intention to deal with the working classes under the headings 'temporal condition, morals, education, and remedy'![96]

Moral failings were partly a matter of working-class capacity for drink. Byng had found himself quite overcome by the noise and drunkenness of the artisans at Salford in 1790, and the *Commercial Directory* of 1816–17, singled out Birmingham for praise for its solitary escape from that 'baneful influence of spiritous liquors which have made dreadful havoc on the population of many other manufacturing districts'.[97] The 'pernicious vice of drinking' was said to be on the increase among the young females of Manchester's cotton factories in 1815, whilst the minister of Arbroath was later to attribute nine tenths of the miseries of the places to improvidence and intemperance.[98] Nor has modern enquiry undermined contemporary views on the high ratio of public houses to private dwellings, or the importance of expenditure on drink in the family budget. Drinking has rather been explained as part of the culture pattern of working-class life, a central function and not a dispensable luxury, and the assault upon drinking habits been interpreted, conversely, as part of the contemporary effort to

73

break up traditional patterns and transform the labouring poor into the working classes, with a new disciplined role to fulfil within industrial society.[99]

Immorality was also, of course, understood to mean sexual immorality. Towns had always had an evil reputation in this matter, and the new factories helped to compound it, for promiscuity was believed to be rife in these establishments. The *Manchester Mercury* deplored the increase of immorality in Lancashire in September 1800, and suggested, perhaps melodramatically, that a 'torrent of vice almost threatens the country with destruction'.[100] The sexual morals of the factory worker received some support from the Factory Commissioners of 1833, who thought they were probably no different from those of other workers outside factories, and one MP, Mr Blamire, even went so far, in March 1832, to argue that the population of the agricultural districts was more immoral, when judged by illegitimacy statistics, than that employed in manufactures.[101] This produced an entertaining slanging match, but no agreement as to the appropriate criteria for assessing relative degrees of immorality within different sub-cultures. Recent findings that illegitimate children were commoner between 1810 and 1850 than at any other time in the nation's past on which information is known, do suggest that the contrasts between rural innocence and urban–industrial corruption had, for once, some basis in fact.[102]

A more generally agreed test for immorality was incidence of attendance at religious worship, and well before the religious census of 1851 had revealed the extent to which the working classes had deserted the churches, it was already clear, in Gaskell's words, that little regard was being paid to religion by the mass of the manufacturing population in the towns, and that most of the mill workers were living 'in practical heathenism'.[103] In part this could be explained, and was explained, by the failure to provide sufficient religious accommodation to keep pace with the growing concentrations of population, but there were always doubts expressed whether religion was any longer capable of making a sufficient appeal to the working classes, for whom, it was said, political reading and speculation were taking over from religion and the Bible.[104] Certainly the new political ferment held out a wide variety of options for industrial and political conduct with which religion found itself struggling to compete and not always successfully. The 1851 religious census confirmed the general suspicion that the working classes, particularly of the northern towns, were little concerned with religious worship, and any remaining doubt on this subject concerns the exact extent of this indifference, not its existence.[105]

But it was not only their failure to attend religious worship that made the colliers and their children an object of concern to the Commissioners on Child Employment in 1842. In the absence of religious and any other form of instruction, the children were simply very ignorant and knew hardly anything.[106] The *Manchester Guardian*'s concern at the 'want of institutions properly adapted to the present state of literature, science, and arts for educating the children of parents in the middle and working classes of society', hardly envisaged the desperate situation of total ignorance and indifference that successive commissioners encountered as they came across rapid accumulations of people in small areas, under no restraint and instruction, and in need of some much more basic and fundamental civilising agency than the *Guardian* seemed to be suggesting.[107] The boys who had never heard of London, America, or an adjacent village were not quite ready for literature or science, and sound behaviour was a first requirement, for its own sake, and then as an essential pre-condition of the cultural attainment which the more optimistic had in mind.[108] But first something had to be done about the way the manufacturers and colliers, of Wolverhampton for instance, spent their Saturday nights. According to the Commissioners on Child Employment in 1842, on this evening the working classes felt a general desire to get rid of the greater part of their week's earnings on carousing and buying in for Sunday. Entertainment was on hand

75

from musicians, dancers, the venders of quack medicines, and those who could describe the latest execution. 'Meantime songs and vociferations are heard in every beer shop and small public-house ... with servant girls struggling in vain to attend to calls, smashing ale-jugs, or emptying them over colliers' frocks. Children are continually emerging from between crowded legs, and running about in all directions.... The chief noise is among the colliers, as the capering activity is entirely with them. ... There are many fights and other street rows towards midnight.'[109]

It was easier to describe and condemn such scenes than suggest a remedy for them, and the occasional sympathetic voice was to be heard explaining the working-class predicament and offering a solution along other than purely repressive lines. No wonder, commented the *Manchester Guardian*, in February 1833, the poor were resorting to the alehouses and the beer-shops, for they had been systematically deprived of all their other forms of amusement.[110] Nor could the break-up of the ale-houses of the poor be regarded as a paternal gesture unless some step were taken to replace them with something else. It was the poverty of the new town's social institutions that allowed the inns and beer-shops their pre-eminent role, and it was up to society's rulers to extend social provision, not to eliminate the little that existed because it was unsatisfactory. The recognition of this problem really comes of age in the 1840s. Prior to that, in the 1830s, John Fielden and James Kay had produced their rival diagnoses of the problem and their rival prescriptions for action, but both with a tendentious commitment to political principle. Kay, who had visited during the 1832 cholera epidemic the 'loathsome haunts of poverty and vice', sadly noted how many of the evils of the poor derived from their own ignorance or moral error, want of sobriety, prudence, industry, and foresight. For him cholera was the clearest demonstration of the consequences of insobriety, uncleanness, improvidence and idleness, and his visits to the houses of squalid poverty and reckless vice only served to demonstrate the arguments in favour of industry and virtue. As an industrious and virtuous man himself, he had no difficulty in laying down these worthy precepts for others to follow: it was the gospel of improvement that he preached as a reformist.[111] John Fielden took a more impassioned view of the situation and had far more radical attitudes. If the accounts of Kay and his friends were correct, if the immense community connected with commerce and manufacturing really exhibited a picture of such appalling vice, wretchedness, soured temper, and degeneracy, then this was the result not of personal moral failings but of the cruelties of the manufacturing system which the palliatives of Sunday schools or clean streets would hardly be sufficient to cure.[112] These two responses, the conservative and the radical, between them embodied much of what society had to offer in the 1840s as a solution to these new problems that confronted it.

But more important than the relative merits of the proferred solutions was the clear awareness in the 1840s that there existed a general problem, that it had been caused by industrialisation and urbanisation, and that it would not solve itself. The shallow approach of some MPs, Villiers and Hume for example in 1840, tried to turn a parliamentary discussion on child labour and the condition of the working classes into an attack on the Corn Laws and an advocacy of free trade, but not all were concerned to make political capital.[113] Immeasurably greater insight came from the Mining Commissioners who reported in 1843, in their discussion of the iron trade, that 'a creation of wealth and population so rapid as that which has resulted from the great extension of the iron manufacture, cannot be expected to occur without attendant evils, demanding the vigilant attention of those to whom the duty is intrusted to adapting the institutions of the country to its ever-changing circumstances and wants.'[114] This was the problem in a nutshell. Again the Mining Commissioners, in 1844, emphasised the very recent growth of industry in most areas, and the unforeseen consequences of growth for those involved in it. The effect on hearts and minds had not been calculated. If it had been, 'it must have been foreseen by the most inevitable process of logical induction, that the circumstances surrounding them must infallibly lead to a great variety of bad consequences, as if those consequences themselves had been expressly intended and wished for. The arduous task has not been adequately met, and the final result is, amidst a scene of great material prosperity, and an abundance of the means of animal enjoyment, a vast amount of social disorganisation and moral degradation. The evils have grown up until they have become too palpable to be misunderstood.'[115] The quality of this kind of observation is rare and of a totally new order.

The second 1842 report by the Commissioners on Child Employment was also a landmark, for it left behind no possible doubt about the existence of a problem. The factories and mines were shown to be not exceptional but typical in their exploitation of children. Commissioners were becoming more sensitive in their responses and severe in their judgments, and governments were being presented with comprehensive accounts of the labour force of the new society which they could ignore only at their peril. And the sanitary reports of the 1840s on the large towns and populous districts confirmed that 'the wealthy and intelligent classes' were, for the most part, now alive to the great question of the physical condition of the poorer inhabitants. To accept the existence of a problem was certainly to take the first step towards its solution.

The workers were talked about and referred to as an accepted and recognisable characteristic of the new society, though their treatment varied enormously depending on who was currently holding forth. According to the sympathetic Disraeli, they were the 'millions of toil' whose own advance in the national scale had borne no due relationship to the progress of their rulers.[116] They were the labouring classes who, according to Coleridge, had acquired the ominously appropriate title of the 'labouring poor'.[117] They were the lowest and largest class, according to Shelley, who produced that others might consume, whilst they themselves ate less bread, wore worse clothes, were more ignorant, miserable, and desperate than all others.[118] When they were driven to it, they might riot, as they did in 1811–12, and their activities would then be reported, Cobbett found, as those of brutes rather than people who had lives and explicable grievances.[119] A brute's existence seems to concur with Sir James Graham's description of the life of a worker as 'eating, drinking, working and dying'.[120]

One step removed from the sympathy of people like Coleridge or Cobbett was the patronage of an MP or the assurance of a leader-writer that the working classes for all their roughness were sound at heart. This was exemplified by the Commons' members who applauded the petition of Leeds woollen workers in 1817 because of their correct constitutional behaviour in framing such a petition, but they never troubled to concern themselves with its contents.[121] Both the *Manchester Guardian* and the *Leeds Mercury* were similarly concerned to show in 1831–2 that the vast majority of the working classes, the respectable elements within them, were solidly behind the government's reform proposals, and that there was little support from within the working-class ranks for 'extremist' proposals for the ballot or manhood suffrage. In practice, this patronage of the respectable working classes and a pretended support for the respectable elements were no more than an exhortation to join middle-class campaigns. All indigenous working-class industrial or political campaigns and their leaders could rely on the sneers and the scorn of the middle-class Liberal press if independent initiative was being asserted.

The common condemnation of such action was that the workers were being duped by their so-called friends. Good workers should always be quiescent and well-behaved, perhaps because working-class suffering was something that the middle-class liberals never really understood, and if they departed from the expected norm—like the Manchester weavers of 1808—they became 'deluded people', 'a large body of misguided and infatuated people' who were unable to discriminate between their real friends, their employers, and the designing persons

79

who artfully misled them for their own purposes, the strike leaders.[122] The sentiment was echoed again in 1831—'the sound and industrious part of the working classes' stood behind the government, whilst 'a most daring conspiracy' was attempted by 'desperate men who seek to dupe the working classes' by displaying violent, inflammatory placards.[123] Over Chartism too, the *Manchester Guardian* seems to have viewed the matter as purely and simply an issue of law and order; the middle-class desire was for social order, and any working-class demand that threatened that must be the work of some self-seeking agitator who was trying to deflect the workers from their proper interest. Such a man was Charlotte Brontë's Moses Barraclough, a leader of the Spen Valley Luddites, who allegedly incited his fellows to outrage for bad purposes of his own, and deliberately exploited working-class distress because he was meddling, impudent, selfish, and ambitious.[124]

The greatest meddlers and the greatest parasites were the trade union leaders, of whom John Doherty enjoyed the *Manchester Guardian*'s principal accolade for complete cynicism, as a man who cared nothing for 'starving specimens', and whose only concern was personal enjoyment, being well paid and well fed.[125] Without education, Dr Kay claimed, the workers became the prey of those who flattered their passions and adopted their prejudices: the delegates and other leaders became, in the words of the *Nottingham Journal*, the leeches which sucked the very heart's blood of the operatives.[126] Trade unions were, in the words of one MP, Mr Hardy, of all curses the most abominable, not just for what they did to the masters, but because of the poor unfortunates who were compelled to join them.[127] They were, according to Andrew Ure, conspiracies of workmen against the interests of their own order, which they tolerated because they were insufficiently conversant with the principles of political economy.[128] A more perceptive, though equally condemnatory, attitude was that of the witness to the 1838 committee on combinations, who considered that the system of trade unionism was just a conspiracy of skilled labour aristocrats against the mass of unskilled labourers.[129] But criticisms rarely showed this kind of penetration. More usually they contained the simple abuse that trade unionists were trouble-makers and well-paid ones at that; indicated regret that British employers did not have the same freedom as some of their continental rivals to ignore trouble-making unionists or throw them into prison; or were the typically nineteenth century response that trade unions were morally pernicious, erecting barriers between masters and men, and rendering workmen improvident. The remedy, according to the usual prescription, was for the workers to disavow all habits and practices which destroyed them physically and morally; the escape from the toils of trade unions was essentially a question of moral reform.

Such lecturing of the working classes was perhaps but one step away from the complete contempt that characterised many references to them, like Sir James Graham's denunciation of the 'set of idle, discontented . . . workmen' who petitioned in 1818 for factory reform, or Butterworth's reference at the same time to the 'most degenerate race of human beings' who were now threatening the social fabric by their emergence.[130] Contempt is, in practice, difficult to distinguish from the fear that coloured attitudes towards those labouring classes, among whom disaffection and the wildest theories were said to prevail in 1841, men who, in the east of Scotland coalfields, lived virtually an animal existence, devoid of religious character or political bias. Workers in the mines of Durham and Northumberland were said to be the 'very scum and offscouring of a peculiar and mischievous and unlettered race', and of the people of Lanarkshire, two thirds were said to be below the level of civilisation attained by the ordinary labouring classes of the country.[131] The relations of the working classes of England to its privileged orders were, according to one of Disraeli's characters in Sybil, relations of enmity and therefore of peril.[132] It would not be difficult to show that the relations of the privileged orders to the working classes were equally those of enmity, though enough of the privileged orders would eventually be sufficiently appreciative of the dangers involved in this to wish to do something to rectify the situation.

This consciousness of hostilities, or consciousness of class was to become increasingly common in the writings of the nineteenth century. A class-divided town of masters and workers, perhaps Manchester by 1820, had been anticipated by the process of social separation in the countryside, the clearer delineation of labourer status, the decline of living-in, and the ending of the old practice, commented upon by the Poor Law Commissioners, of the servant taking his victuals at his master's table.[133] The Commissioners on Handloom Weaving in 1840–1, commented upon the altered social relationships observable in agriculture as well as in manufacture, but they regretted particularly the absentee manufacturer and the weakened bond between the employer and his outworkers.[134] The physical separation of the social classes in the manufacturing districts was noted by Stuart Wortley, one of Yorkshire's MPs in 1819, when he referred to the non-residence of persons of wealth and rank within these areas.[135] It was becoming increasingly the practice for second-generation factory owners to move away from the town centres, leaving, according to George Taylor in 1833, the operatives and their families in the immediate vicinity of their machines, whilst the masters fled to the suburbs or the rural parishes, thereby escaping the consequences, aesthetic and financial, of the factories they had installed.[136]

Yet the factory owners seemed models of social responsibility when compared to the coal and iron owners of the early 1840s, who created a disastrous impression upon those who investigated the communities for which they were responsible. Symons found the Yorkshire mine owners indifferent to their responsibilities, and the upper classes in general devoid of any sense of obligation to the workers.[137] Thomas Tancred discovered in Coatbridge a society entirely made up of colliers and iron-workers, with no gentry or middle class to leaven the mix.[138] In Northumberland and Durham, Franks commented on the entire absence of resident gentry, and explained how and why they moved out of an area as soon as industry moved in, whilst the Mining Commissioners were still dwelling in 1843 on the exclusion from their areas of all visitors save those whose daily bread depended on their residence.[139] The development of the butty system of middlemen was tending to break the connections between the employers and the workmen, and the absentee profiteer was simply abdicating all social responsibility. Truck, even, was serving to check the growth of a middle class of traders and thereby reducing the civilising influence a middle-class presence might have brought to the mining areas.[140]

What was in fact growing up was the widely recognised and widely lamented practice of wealthy men refusing to accept the obligations that traditionally were supposed to accompany the possession of wealth. Now wealth was on the increase. The 'unmitigated exercise of the calculating faculty', according to Shelley, must ever result in the rich becoming richer and the poor becoming poorer.[141] This nation was, in Cobbett's view, coming to consist of a few very rich and millions of very poor, whilst Carlyle was to support the notion that wealth was gathering itself into masses and increasing the distance between the rich and the poor.[142] But this was irresponsible wealth. Just as the Commissioners on Child Employment regretted, in 1842, the absence of a sense of obligation among the employing classes, so did Disraeli's young Coningsby perceive that wealth was rapidly developing classes whose duties in the social system seemed altogether omitted. Robert Owen lamented the frittering away of ties between employers and their workers and their concern only with what immediate gain each could derive from the other. All was now being done by rule and calculated contrivance, said Carlyle, with 'cash payment as the sole nexus'.[143]

The new towns seemed best to exemplify this new calculation and separation, especially Manchester, which Dr Spiker visited in 1816. He passed through an agreeable part as he approached from the south, through the dwellings of the proprietors of the manufactures, and commented that the workers themselves were to be found elsewhere.[144] This principle was well illustrated by Cooke Taylor's aphorism in the early 1840s that, 'Ardwick knows less about Ancoats than it does about China and feels more interest in the condition of New Zealand than of Little Ireland', and it provoked an attack from Engels on the hypocritical planning of a town which kept its working-class and middle-class districts quite distinct.[145] This was the area where class feelings are thought to have been most developed; one modern authority, for instance, suggests that it was commonplace by 1820 to explain the basic social and political differences within society by the economic divisions between owners and workers, and he quotes a contemporary press statement that there was 'no sympathy between upper and lower classes of society'.[146] On the whole, modern commentators are disinclined to generalise on this subject, and prefer to stress the different experiences of different places, determined by the nature of local industry, the structure of the employing group, and the occupational make-up of the labour force in particular towns. Thus the cotton towns have seemed to be places of class-consciousness and class-conflict, whilst the light-engineering and steel centres of Birmingham and Sheffield avoided such stark confrontations, and individual factors have been identified in smaller towns such as St Helens, South Shields, and Northampton to explain the retarded class-consciousness observed in these industrial centres.[147]

The whole concept of class and class-consciousness is most complicated and defies the application of agreed criteria in attempts that have been made to establish its existence, but there is no doubt that people were beginning to use the language of class and supply it with a meaning derived from the new industrial context in which it was being employed. Owen, for instance, had suggested that society was now divided into classes which were not bound by reciprocal obligation but by the impersonal ties of the market, a clear attempt to relate the term to a new economic structure.[148] William Cobbett went further in describing the conflict over general unionism in 1833-4 as 'one class of society united to oppose another class', and suggested that the nation had been very nearly divided into two classes, 'the idle living chiefly on the taxes, in one way or another, and the industrious, who have their earnings taken from them to maintain the idlers'.[149] But this was crude and a possible radical critique of any society rather than the one which confronted Cobbett with all its qualifications and ramifications. Howitt broke down Cobbett's picture a little when he approached agriculture and manufactures separately but suggested that a common pattern of 'the great capitalist and the slave' would soon apply equally to both areas.[150] It would take Engels and Marx to identify many of the refinements within both the 'capitalist' and the 'slave' class, but Engels was already identifying in the 1840s a separate working class supposedly conscious of its own existence, a phenomenon to engross many generations of future scholars as they strove to elucidate the precise social consequences of the Industrial Revolution.[151]

Though contemporaries were increasingly if vaguely aware of the largely alarming working classes who were at the base of the new economic system, they were more clearly aware, with a different kind of alarm, that 'new orders of men had arisen in the country, new sources of wealth had opened, new dispositions of power'.[152] These were not simply the middle-class industrialists who might seem the easiest to identify. For Shelley, the new aristocracy was one of 'attornies, and excisemen and directors, government pensioners, usurers, stocking-jobbers, country-bankers, with dependants and descendants', a list very similar in composition and character to Cobbett's villainous fund-holders, contractors, and sinecurists.[153] Cobbett did, of course, add the 'Seigneurs of the Twist, sovereigns of the Spinning Jenny, great yeomen of the Yarn', an 'abominable crew of upstarts' who conspired 'to support their injustice and tyranny', but it is interesting to note that in their role of public villains the industrialists were preceded by a generation of financiers, and it was the latter who first provoked attacks upon the new spirit of commercialism that had entered national life.[154]

'New orders of men' suggested social mobility, and it was, as the mill owner, Mr Thornton, told the young lady in *North and South*, 'one of the great beauties of our system that a working-man may raise himself into the power and position of a master by his own exertions and behaviour.'[155] There had been the most extraordinary opportunities over the past thirty-six years, reported the *Manchester Guardian* in 1833, for men to raise themselves above their original status, and the cotton industry was celebrated for its quickly made fortunes.[156] Indeed, an examination of the petitions of Scottish handloom weavers in 1834, revealed the surprising information that two late Lord Provosts of Glasgow had risen from the ranks of cotton weavers.[157] Seven years later, the Commissioners on Handloom Weaving were still holding out hopes that a few labourers might raise themselves into the capitalist ranks, but conceded that this could happen in only a very few cases.[158] In fact the much publicised gospel of improvement and self-help served only to obscure the very limited prospects and achievements of the self-made men within early and later Victorian society, and investigations of the steel and hosiery industries, for instance, have shown how little recruitment occurred from the ranks of the workers to those of the entrepreneurs.[159]

The rising social forces were not, on the whole, the enterprising industrious workmen from the ranks, but the historians' friends, the middle classes, 'the middling and most useful class of the community', according to the *Manchester Mercury* in 1806, men moderate yet firm in all their opinions, possessing, in Lord Althorp's view, in 1831, a higher degree of character and intelligence than at any former period, for he clearly saw them as no entirely new phenomenon.[160] As men of commercial and manufacturing property they were alternately demanding the political power to which their wealth entitled them, and craving the political exemptions that their poverty made necessary. On the one hand the *Manchester Guardian* might ask why this or that earl should have twenty times the power of the inhabitants of Manchester in returning members to Parliament, when these inhabitants possessed fifty times the wealth of the two noblemen together; this was a pragmatic, no-nonsense approach to the realities of social change and political representation.[161] At the same time the legislature was alleged to be so ignorant of all matters relating to industry that it repeatedly brought manufacture to the very brink of destruction by its wrong-headed commercial policies and excessive taxation.

The picture that emerges of the manufacturing interests, of the north of England at least, is of a highly self-conscious interest group, at once smug and complacent, yet self-pitying for the risk that it took and the poverty that it so narrowly escaped. It had a capacity, almost exceeding that of the landowners, for confusing its own with the national interest, yet, in the words of George Eliot's Felix Holt, 'most of the middle class are as ignorant as the work people about everything that doesn't belong to their own Brummagen life.'[162] Way back in 1785 William Pitt had informed Parliament that the cotton manufacturers had become so important that even their errors and prejudices needed serious consideration.[163] Within half a century these 'errors and prejudices' were determining national policy, and laying down new purposes for governments to follow. With acute perception, the *Manchester Guardian*, in October 1831, offered the opponents of reform a deal whereby, if they would give their assent to reform, they would themselves be given protection from the revolutionaries—as shrewd and prophetic an appraisal of the social situation as it is possible to find in these years.[164]

This realignment of social forces, this new alliance of landed and industrial interests against the working classes, was more real than apparent during the first half of the nineteenth century, when the arguments between the two sides seemed to rage fiercely across an unbridgeable gulf. They first acquired great heat during the debates that preceded and accompanied the Corn Law of 1815, which seemed to many MPs an odious piece of class legislation selfishly imposed by one section of the community upon the rest. Prior to that, talk of the 'common interest' had generally prevailed, and there had been a widespread tendency to see the manufacturing industries as a 'good thing' because they contributed substantially to the wealth and strength of the nation. From the Corn Law debates onwards the arguments multiplied and the divisions became evident. By the operation of the new law, argued the *Nottingham Review*, the farmers would become direct tax-gatherers upon the commercial, manufacturing, and monied interests, filling the pockets of the landed proprietors.[165] The landed interests had enjoyed considerable prosperity during the war, which they had not passed on to their tenants, argued the *Manchester Guardian*; now the community as a whole was being taxed for their private profit. It was not, said the editor, that he wished to be thought hostile to the land, but, as he had repeatedly said, the country owed its difficulties principally to the landed interest.[166] They, according to Lord Milton, were responsible for the iniquitous taxes on raw wool on the one hand, and the unfair easy export of long wool from Britain on the other, policies designed to favour the wool-growers, the landed interest, and damage the manufacturers, policies which were losing contracts for Britain, such as that to clothe the Russian army.[167] If Parliament were not careful and did not listen to the voice of the manufacturers, Great Britain was in danger of losing a large part of her overseas trade, said Sir Evelyn Baring in 1821.[168] What the landed interest were in fact doing, according to the *Leeds Mercury*, was monopolising political power and abusing it to further their own interest, not only in the partial legislation that they framed, but in their wasteful and extravagant fixing of establishment salaries, showing a 'high-bred contempt for money' which was anathema to those who held it in such reverence.[169] The country owed everything to its men of commerce and manufacture, stated Sir George Villiers in 1837, yet their interests and the national interest were being sacrificed to those of an unproductive class.[170] And in the debates that preceded the repeal of the Corn Laws in 1846 the propaganda of the Anti-Corn Law League succeeded in fixing firmly the image of 'oafish, indolent aristocrats'.[171]

The argument was not, of course, entirely one-sided, as saddened MPs endeavoured to persuade their rivals in debate just what they owed to the land. Mr Brand, for instance, in February 1815, listed the services of the landowners during the late war in making and preserving highways, maintaining the clergy, supporting the poor, including the manufacturing poor, and keeping the soldiers' wives![172] The Marquis of Chandos pursued the same theme in 1837 when he claimed credit for the agricultural interests for maintaining the country despite its debts, keeping the peace of the country, and in general keeping the country going in wartime.[173] The landed interest had their fears as did the manufacturers; they feared that, exposed to natural hazards and without the assistance of complex machinery, the farmer, without protection, could not fairly be expected to survive; they feared that parliamentary reform would bring together such a formidable alliance of middle and working classes, that property would lose all its former preponderance; they feared too, that the manufacturing interest would exploit that alliance to destroy completely the influence of the landed aristocracy; and they feared that the repeal of the Corn Laws was intended to ruin agriculture so that agricultural labourers would be driven to the towns to create a cheap labour force for the manufacturers.[174] All these fears, rational or otherwise, led them towards as bitter an invective upon the manufacturers as had been let loose against themselves. The new industrialists became 'machine-owning vampires' and 'monsters of covetousness', and the manufacturing capitalists were accused of creating the total pauperism of the country.[175]

It is more than a little ironical that those who sought to heal these breaches with soothing platitudes, which they probably did not believe most of the time, came nearer to an accurate appraisal of the social balance and an accurate forecast of the outcome of the contest, than those who spoke the language of class warfare. Many MPs endeavoured to cool down the debate. Ellison, who described the people of England as 'one great united body', Flood, who believed that the interests of agriculturists and manufacturers went hand-in-hand, and Redesdale, who thought it nothing less than libellous to set landholder and manufacturer against each other, all attempted to calm the mood in 1815.[176] When Stuart Wortley MP, addressed a Bradford wool dinner in 1824, proposing the toast of the 'Agricultural and Commercial Interests of the United Kingdom', his position called for the greatest tact and diplomacy, and he wisely maintained on this occasion that neither could flourish without the other, though on other occasions there were constituents who found it difficult to reconcile his benign sentiments with his support for the Corn Laws.[177] As Lord John Russell intimated to the House of Commons during the early stages of the debates on the reform of Parliament, there had of late years been a strong degree of suspicion and jealousy between the landed and commercial interests, one which he was concerned to eliminate.[178] And it is one of the most remarkable features of nineteenth century British history that both the Reform Act of 1832, and the Repeal of the Corn Laws in 1846, should have been accomplished with such minimal disturbance to the existing social balance; that such essential harmony should have in fact prevailed when there were so many vociferous testimonies to the disharmony bred of an apparently irreconcilable conflict of interest.

But until this essential harmony could be successfully demonstrated, as it was in the middle years of the century, proclamations on its behalf were little more than pious hopes or outrageous hypocrisy, according to viewpoint. Robert Owen's belief in the structural unity of society was taking some hard knocks from competitive industry, and these were hardly to be softened by the member who informed Parliament in 1806 that manufacturers, employers and employed alike had the same interest, to promote the growth and prosperity of manufactures.[179] The idea was persistently advocated, and remains popular, that the interests of the working classes and their employers were 'precisely identical'; on the question of hours, argued the *Manchester Guardian*, as in all other matters, there was a common identity of interest which should be pursued without legislative interference.[180] This proposition is at least worthy of continued debate, unlike that collector's piece from the Assistant-Commissioner on Handloom Weaving, who unctuously recorded that 'inequality of fortune' was 'inevitable and beneficial even to the lowest classes in a healthy community'.[181]

That this doctrine was not a source of universal comfort is amply testified by the growing sense of alarm experienced by the people of Great Britain in the 1830s and the early 1840s as they surveyed the new society that was coming into being and wondered what it held in store for them. From the want of an efficient preventive force, argued the Constabulary Commissioners in 1839, the peace and the manufacturing prosperity had become exposed to considerable danger, but the danger did not exist simply in the administrative breakdown, greatly as that exacerbated it.[182] Crowds had always been fearful things, and crowds were now bigger and more concentrated than ever, and motivated by grievances and desires which the rulers of society were hardly beginning to understand. In 1819, Henry Brougham commented on the separation between the higher and lower orders of society, a state of things which he believed could end only in the destruction of liberty, or convulsion which would produce the same result.[183] This pessimism affected at times even the classical economists, the apostles of economic growth, who, in times of crisis exhibited what has been described as 'grave, even hysterical anxiety at the restlessness of the people'.[184] The social novels of the 1840s contain the strong theme of fear that the working classes would take matters into their own hands, and domestic convulsion was widely seen as the probable outcome of the social situation that Britain was in by 1840. This fear is perhaps best illustrated by Cooke Taylor's vision in 1841 of a population gathering strength to produce 'something portentous and fearful', like 'the slow rising and gradual swelling of an ocean which must, at some future and no distant time, bear all the elements of society aloft upon its bosom, and float them—Heaven knows whither.'[185] That such an alarming prospect did not materialise was the result of a great work of reform and reconciliation which somehow permitted the old society to absorb the new without the intervention of revolution, not the least achievement of the Industrial Revolution in Great Britain.

Notes to this chapter are on page 173.

4 The New Values

If the Industrial Revolution meant dramatic changes in the countryside, new patterns of work and new habits of life, it also meant the acceptance, and then the questioning, of new values for society, new ideas by which people lived and had their being. In particular, it meant the emergence of contrasting social ideals, and rival notions of how society ought to be organised, which have supplied the enduring content of practically the whole of the political debate that has taken place over two centuries.

One of these social ideals, known by a variety of names, of which liberalism and individualism are perhaps the most familiar, derived from the doctrines of political economy, found in the works of the classical economists, Adam Smith and his successors, who were concerned to discover and explain the laws of economic life. These doctrines resembled God's commandments to Moses, in that although they arrived at some historical point in time, they nevertheless contained eternal truths. As Ricardo informed the House of Commons in 1823, with all the authority of the current high-priest, the principles of true political economy never changed, and those who did not understand the science should say nothing about it.[1] The principles never changed, but they had not always been known. 'We are well aware', stated the *Manchester Guardian* in January 1822, that '. . . in the infancy of our commerce, and before the dawn of political science various laws were past [*sic*] for the protection . . .' of industry which ceased to be operative when their folly became understood.[2] William Pitt the Younger was one of the first statesmen to experience this new dawn. In a much quoted speech in 1796, he argued that trade, industry, and barter must be free to find their own level, and, with the conviction of a zealot that all around him shared his views, stated that it was unnecessary for him to go into the argument of the general inexpediency of legislative interference in economic affairs. This had been demonstrated both by the 'celebrated writers on political economy', and by that great teacher, experience.[3] The human derivation of these ideas was not always accepted by later figures, who saw them as a divine contribution to Britain's commercial triumph in the nineteenth-century world, and Richard Oastler's attack on the 'allegedly immutable laws of economics' recognised, and at the same time criticised, their elevated status in the faith and dogma of a nation.[4] When John Wright, a magistrate of Thetford in Norfolk, communicated to the Poor Law Commissioners about the unemployment that had resulted locally from the introduction of machinery, he was very quick to assure them that he was fully aware that 'it is not in the power of the legislature to correct the evil'.[5] To have believed otherwise would have been to entertain heresy.

Works of learned philosophy or profound economic analysis rarely become the basis of commonly held views as a result of the mass readership they acquire. Their ideas are invariably transmitted through popularising agents who reduce them to simpler, more understandable forms, leaving them more crude and unsophisticated than their founders ever intended. Just as Karl Marx could hardly be blamed for all that has been attributed to him by his interpreters and followers, so too would it be wrong to hold Smith, Ricardo, Malthus, McCulloch or Nassau Senior responsible for the popular versions of their teachings disseminated by the cheap tracts of Harriet Martineau, as for example in her *Illustrations of Political Economy*. The provincial press of the manufacturing areas, such as the *Leeds Mercury*, Westminster politicians, or Lancashire industrialists, were all likely to push certain doctrines to the limit and argue for unrestrained economic individualism or even total non-interference in social matters, on the basis of what they supposed to be the teachings of the political economists. For their part, the classical economists were invariably less rigid in their attitudes, less united in their views, and more influenced by the pressure of events than was commonly supposed, though what was commonly supposed was the stuff of the contemporary political debate rather than what was originally written or actually said.[6]

A not unreasonable distillation of the teachings of the economists came from a witness who gave evidence to a Select Committee on Silk Weavers' Petitions in 1818, when he expressed his belief that 'every regulation which interferes with a manufacture is useless, hurtful, and dangerous. It unsettles the workmen, repels the artist, blunts industry, disgusts the consumer, discredits the seller, and ruins the enterprise.'[7] Political economy often seemed like a charter of manufacturer's rights to pursue his business without restriction in whatever way he thought best, and his basic right, as enunciated by the 1806 Select Committee on the Wool Trade, was the right to employ his capital freely; this particular statement was made to justify the new woollen factories which aroused the opposition of the workmen and small manufacturers, but which were defended in terms of the capitalist's need to experiment and to speculate and his freedom to do so.[8] And part of this freedom and right to employ capital to his own advantage was the freedom to invest in machinery. It was lamentable, commented the *Manchester Guardian*, in March 1822, that there should still exist a prejudice against the employment of machinery.[9] This prejudice, which gave certain branches of the textile trades some very stormy episodes in their history, was thought to disregard the practical advantages to be derived from the application of machinery and to deny the right of the manufacturer to pursue the course that would bring him the greatest profit and the community the greatest benefit. Such a denial was contrary to the precepts of political economy.

The manufacturer's next concern was with labour supply,

and this again should be available to him without control or restraint. When Sir Robert Peel the Elder and Robert Owen led the demand for restrictions on the laws of child labour, they were told that the cotton owners objected to 'interference with free labour' and were opposed to 'propositions to interfere with them in the conduct of their own business'.[10] Such proposals were also, said Mr Curwen, in 1816, a libel on the humanity of parents as well as an infringement of their liberty, since they aimed to regulate the parental authority over what a child could bear.[11] When, at a later stage, proposals were made to limit the working day in factories to ten hours, this was widely condemned as an intolerable interference with labour supply and with the freedom of the subject. Not all the political economists were so hostile to factory reform as Nassau Senior, who strongly opposed the Ten Hour Movement, and, by the 1840s, arguments of social necessity were becoming increasingly acceptable to those who continued to support non-interference in matters of purely economic concern. Yet the freedom of contract required by political economy undoubtedly impeded the progress of the factory movement.[12]

Another aspect of labour supply concerned the free movement of labour inside and outside the country. Although some manufacturers had strong reservations about the right of skilled artisans to emigrate, the logic of non-interference was successfully pressed by Francis Place and Joseph Hume in 1824, and the *Leeds Mercury* conceded that it would be as unjust to prevent a man from selling his labour in the best market as it would to prevent an employer from buying his on the best terms.[13] It was easier for the manufacturers to welcome the aim of the Poor Law of 1834 to move the surplus labour of the South East into the manufacturing areas of the Midlands and North where there was a demand for it. The commissioners quoted with approval the opinions of the Rev A. B. Hennibear, Chairman of the Hartismere Union, who argued that the freedom of labour to move to the market would bring a benefit to both employer and the employed so obvious as not to require comment; the long established traditions that a man could look to his parish for subsistence was a 'deep-rooted error, fostering all pauperism', and Adam Smith had been right in his judgment that the Law of Settlement was the 'severest and most unjust law ever imposed on the industry of the labouring classes in any civilised country'; the unemployed should go where work was available and not have a right to be supported where it was not.[14] And if work in a particular trade, weaving for example, was not available anywhere, weavers were free to change their occupation and to control their own reproductive processes.

Closely associated with the question of labour supply was that of wages, for the one assuredly determined the other. There could be no artificial interference for the fixing of wages by criteria other than the availability of labour for a job. Again, the trade of the cotton handloom weaver is probably the best illustration of the principle at work. As the trade became flooded with unskilled labour, and weavers found themselves in competition with power-looms, the demand for their services fell and their wages declined from 1800 onwards. They attempted to halt this trend by campaigns for a legal minimum wage, but these were unsuccessful. They were told in 1803 that if a minimum wage had been granted to spinners in their temporary distress thirty years earlier, the cotton trade would not have reached its existing proportions.[15] Such a concession, it was argued in 1808, would be harmful to manufacturers and workmen alike because it would be harmful to the trade.[16] The general cry, said a sympathetic Bolton manufacturer in 1834, was that Parliament would do nothing for the weavers: and the cry was correct, for according to the *Manchester Guardian*, the legislature was not simply unwilling but rather unable to do anything in this matter.[17] It was not Parliament's sphere; labour had found its own level and it would be absurd to keep it 'factitiously' above this level.

Apart from parliamentary regulation, the other principal means for the artificial fixing of wages which was strongly

97

criticised was that of combination, for this was believed to involve a double coercion, that of employers by workers and that of workers by fellow-workers. The editor of the *Manchester Guardian* indicated the orthodox view on this question when he attacked combinations but at the same time supported 'the right to bargain freely'. He had earlier suggested that the worker possessed the right to refuse work in the same way that the employer possessed the right to refuse employment to those who sought it.[18] It was up to the individual worker and employer to reach a mutually satisfactory arrangement about terms of employment; in doing so both would be enjoying and exercising their liberty. This condemnation of the principle of combination came, however, to be balanced by the liberal economists with a somewhat ironical, if logical, condemnation of the Combination Laws, which were repealed in 1824. Francis Place, though a trade unionist of some energy in his early days, came to believe that trade unions were undesirable, and he thought that by working for the repeal of the Combination Laws he would remove a main incentive to their formation and rid industrial relations of the undesirable presence of the law in their midst. In 1805 an MP had attacked the Laws as an improper interference by the state in economic affairs, a flaw in the new economic logic, and the *Leeds Mercury*, a leading proponent of this logic, was to reject them as 'unjust, useless, and mischievous'.[19] The legislation of 1824–5 left workers with the acknowledged right to combine, but denied them the means to do so effectively, so paying lip-service to the liberties and freedom of the workers, especially those who did not wish to join trade unions, whilst at the same time preserving the freedom of employers from effective combination amongst their workmen. This was by no means the only such case of compromise where the enigmatic principle of freedom needed to be enforced.

Further insidious infringements of the true principles for calculating wages occurred through the operation of the old Poor Law. When a group of weavers petitioned Parliament in

1811 to relieve them in their distress, they were told that Parliament was opposed to the granting of money to alleviate distress since this would destroy 'the equilibrium of labour and employment'.[20] In fact, the equilibrium was repeatedly threatened by all those parishes which supplemented wages by allowances, and in some areas, such as Nottingham, the Poor Law officers were accused of undercutting respectable manufacturers by employing pauper labour and entering into unfair competition with local businessmen.[21] The poor rate was described by Dr Kay in 1834 as 'a tax on capital', and until the law was amended in that year and brought into line with current economic thinking, it permitted a whole range of infringements of the new orthodoxy.[22]

Ideally, Malthus and Ricardo would have scrapped the Poor Laws completely for as long as poor relief of any sort was allowed, an artificial inducement to population growth was retained. The Act of 1834 illustrates how the political economists might have had to accept a qualified application of their theory where expediency demanded this, though they did achieve a situation whereby no pauper was maintained beyond the level of the worst paid member of the work force, which went far towards removing the damaging effects of poor relief on wages.[23] Even before this, in an unconsciously frank acknowledgement of the effect of free enterprise on wages, the *Leeds Mercury* conceded in October 1830, that 'the competition of trade is perpetually operating to induce and almost to compel masters to exact the greatest possible labour from the work people'.[24] In other words, liberty and freedom for both parties to the bargain meant, in effect, that the employers were extorting very severe terms which their workmen had little power to resist.

The greatest and most sought after right for the manufacturers of the Industrial Revolution was the right to free trade, with all the advantages that Adam Smith had described as arising from it when he published *The Wealth of Nations* in 1776. Although the Younger Pitt was supposedly a convert to the ideas of Smith, and reputedly understood their implications even better than Smith himself, and although a committee of enquiry into the woollen trade could report in 1806 on 'the different principles of commerce which are now recognised', this recognition came more from the speeches of MPs than from the law of the land, which remained selectively but heavily protectionist until the 1840s.[25] In 1820 Ricardo expressed his astonishment that the principles of Adam Smith should have taken such a time to be put forward, and even when they had become the currency of the day, there were still duties on raw cotton, monopolies for the East India Company, preferences for colonial sugar, and, above all, prohibitive Corn Laws, showing how slowly the practice of government was catching up with the theory that was so widely expounded.[26] When the *Leeds Mercury* delivered its ultimate condemnation of Cobbett in 1830 on the ground that 'he also ignorantly attacks Free Trade', Huskisson's reciprocal agreements, colonial preferences, and sliding scales had left Great Britain far short of the free trade society that the *Mercury* sought.[27] The Corn Laws, for instance, embodied the wisdom of the nation's governors, Tory or Whig, for a further sixteen years.

But if free trade was the manufacturer's ideal, it was a curiously selective application of the principle that many of them sought. The Younger Pitt had encountered highly sensitive areas of vested interest amongst the manufacturers with his liberal commercial proposals for Ireland back in the 1780s, and it repeatedly happened that the general principle would be supported whilst a specific application of it might be opposed by a particular interest that felt itself threatened. William Wilberforce observed with some irony in 1815 that some 150 articles were prohibited from entry to the country to afford a large measure of protection to native manufactured goods, and the manufacturers raised no outcry over this infringement.[28] Indeed, back in 1785 the Marquis of Landsdowne had suggested that the manufacturers had only two basic ideas, both of them involving monopolies, of raw materials and of the home market.[29] One monopoly which they stoutly defended against the doctrinal purists was that machinery invented inside Britain was prevented by law from being exported until the 1824 Committee on Artisans and Machinery made some inroads into the monopoly. The columns of the *Manchester Mercury* repeatedly contained references to this issue; in February 1800, the paper gleefully reported the case of a man who had been fined £200 and sent to prison for a year for shipping cotton machinery abroad; in February 1803, it reported as 'so great a crime', the procuring of machine models for foreigners to copy; in January 1815, it carried one of its periodic warnings against foreigners who were visiting Lancashire factories engaged in industrial espionage; and later that year it reported attempts that were being made to entice skilled workmen to go to America and take their skills and secrets with them.[30] Against this, Place, Hume, and other free traders argued that the preservation of this monopoly, besides being contrary to the general principle of non-interference, was practically harmful and robbed the country of a considerable export trade in machinery. The government compromised on the principle in 1824, permitted some machines to go and allowed others to remain protected, but even the protected categories found their way out when the demand for them existed, and when the would-be monopolists, the hosiers and lace-manufacturers of Nottingham, for example, attempted to enforce the law they received little co-operation from the authorities.[31]

A further classic case of special pleading was the argument of the early 1820s between the supposedly free-trading woollen manufacturers of the West Riding, who wished to retain a monopoly of home-grown long wool, and the 'growers' who wished to export it freely. Again, when personal interest was threatened a principle collapsed. It was easier to be indignant about the East India Company's trading monopoly or the privileged position of British corn-growers, than to remain perfectly consistent where all matters of trade were concerned.

It might then be thought that political economy, which commended guide-lines of business conduct so favourable to the manufacturer, and such departures from those guide-lines as individuals were occasionally inclined to make, were determined by selfish considerations, that political economy was in fact a rationalisation of self-aggrandisement. It would at least be fair to argue, and more accurate chronologically, that the widespread popularity and acceptance of some of its principal ideas occurred because they produced a philosophical defence of policies that seemed necessary and attractive to merchants and manufacturers in the context of the industrial changes that were taking place. Adam Smith had no intention that the liberalising of trade and industry should operate in favour of the sectional interests of the merchants or manufacturers; he believed in a harmony of interests between producer and consumer, but was concerned that the consumer's should take precedence over the producer's where monopolies threatened injury.[32] His disciple Ricardo did not share this optimism, but most advocates of laissez-faire in economic affairs believed that it was a common interest they were defending, even to the extent of anticipating international peace with the removal of artificial tariff barriers between nations. Internally, the principles of political economy were believed to be a sure basis for national prosperity and eternal felicity. The cotton manufacturers, for instance, saw themselves as benefactors of the entire nation, and by 1804 the prosperity of the cotton trade was already being offered to Parliament as the 'best proof of non-interference'.[33] Later attempts to argue that this success was being achieved at the expense of the working classes were strongly refuted in the *Manchester Guardian* by the classic optimist case that all efforts should be directed towards increasing the productive power of industry; the more commodities produced, the greater the prosperity for all, for mass production demanded mass consumption as Smith had himself insisted.[34] This was political economy as a gospel of progress, optimistic, almost altruistic.

Yet this same set of ideas and principles was described by Michael Sadler, the factory reformer, as 'an ignorant and selfish system of spurious political economy'.[35] Cobbett too delighted in exposing what he believed to be the sheer hypocrisy of the whole network of ideas, citing, for example, the support given by the British to South American freedom so that the independent countries of Latin America would be free to buy British cottons produced in conditions of near slavery in unemancipated Lancashire.[36] Southey rejected the notion that political economy was concerned with general welfare, and condemned its exclusion of all moral considerations.[37] To Richard Oastler it was no more than 'enlightened selfishness', and it seemed nothing less than blasphemy to him that such a principle should be seen, as he believed it was being seen, as the fulfilment of the laws of nature.[38] It seemed to be accepted that if liberty were to be applied to all aspects of economic life, society would look after itself. It was enough that each individual should pursue his private gain for the public good to result without any direction or regulation on behalf of some social purpose. These ideas were to Oastler quite intolerable, if only because they were in practice operating so unjustly, conspicuously favouring 'the privileged and capitalist classes' and not conveying equal benefits over the whole of society.[39] It was not, of course, simply their practical outcome to which Oastler objected, but more fundamentally to the absence of moral purpose that underlay them, and he himself suggested both a moral purpose and an alternative philosophy as he and others rebelled against the qualities and values which the new economics seemed to be encouraging.

The first one to emerge was that identified by the Lakeland poets as 'commercialism', with which they associated 'materialism', both of which were held in equal abhorrence. When he visited Manchester in 1807, Southey found commerce 'the queen witch', and reported that he possessed 'no talisman strong enough to disenchant those who were daily drinking of the golden cup of her charms'; commerce meant that 'everyone endeavours to purchase at the lowest price and sell at the highest, regardless of equity in either case', for business had lost its moral content.[40] Coleridge too identified what he called an 'over-balance of commercial spirit'. His praise for the perfection of mechanical inventions suggests that he was no crude opponent of industrialisation, but rather a critic of the need always to produce the largest and quickest return on capital, to allow sentiment no place in business transactions, and to make mathematical calculation the sole criterion of judgment.[41] Quantitative assessments were everywhere replacing qualitative ones, and human enjoyment was surrendering to 'animal comforts' which, according to Wordsworth, were now being rejoiced over as if they were the end of being.[42]

From within the business world, Robert Owen acknowledged that pecuniary gain was the governing principle of trade, commerce, and manufacture. To achieve this a man must buy cheap and sell dear, and to succeed in this he must acquire such powers of deception that he must lose all honesty and sincerity, the only basis for happiness for himself and those with whom he dealt.[43] 'To acquire, to accumulate, to plunder each other by virtue of philosophic phrases . . . this', according to Disraeli in 1844, had been 'the breathless business of enfranchised England for the last twelve years'.[44] All was concerned with profit and accumulation, even, according to Carlyle, the practising of religion, which he described as a 'wise, prudential policy grounded on mere calculation'.[45] Commercialism was everywhere, the spiritual interests of society, according to John Stuart Mill, were ignored, and this was having a most injurious influence on the national character.[46] It was a good thing, conceded Howitt, that two blades were growing where previously there had been but one, but humanity had needs beyond the physical ones, and provision must be made for the spiritual and intellectual as well as the bodily needs.[47]

The implications of this kind of criticism stretched out in many directions, one of which was educational reform. Another was the need for men to sit down and think out what kind of society they wanted and what order of priorities they had in mind. If it really was a question simply of maximising profit John Ruskin could envisage,

> the whole of the island . . . set as thick with chimneys as the masts stand in the docks of Liverpool; that there shall be no meadows in it; no trees; no gardens; only a little corn grown upon the house tops, reaped and thrashed by steam: that you do not have even room for roads, but travel either over the roofs of your mills, on viaducts; or under their floors, in tunnels; that, the smoke having rendered the light of the sun unserviceable, you work always by the light of your own gas: that no acre of English ground shall be without its shaft and its engine.[48]

This was the debate on commercialism as it would present itself to Ruskin in extreme and nightmarish form in 1859.

At a more personal and homely level it was represented by the imaginary conversation between the weaver and his master recounted by the radical weaver from Middleton, Samuel Bamford. The master, having referred to the new dogma that the great principle of commerce is to buy in the cheapest and sell in the dearest market, explains why he rejects this mode of conduct:

> It is not honest—it is not Christian like—it is not wise. Let us try this vaunted principle, William, by the test of honesty—by the test of 'Do thou unto others as thou wouldest they should do unto thee', and there is no better test of right and wrong under heaven. Suppose thou and thy family were distressed from want of employment and thou came to me asking for work—and I, knowing thy situation, purchased thy labour 'at the cheapest rate at which I could get it', and sold it again at the dearest, putting the profit screwed out of thy necessities into my pocket— suppose I did so,—should I be acting like a Christian?— like an honest, conscientious man?'[49]

The rhetorical question commanded a negative reply, but the complaint of the critics of the new commercialism was that moral considerations, of the kind referred to by the weaver's master, played no part in modern day business transactions, whatever the economists supposed about the moral basis of their ideas.

This same propensity to ignore moral considerations is elsewhere identified as irresponsibility on the part of the employers of the new society. Oastler condemned what he called the 'insane notion' that there was no natural tie between the soil and the people, that property had no duties, and that man had no natural rights.[50] He agreed with Southey's lament that the principle of duty had been weakened and that of moral obligation destroyed.[51] When God gave a blessing to be enjoyed, said Job Legh in *Mary Barton*, it was accompanied by a duty to be done, and the duty of the happy was to help the suffering to bear their woe.[52] The factory masters, said John Fielden, who was one of them, should act towards their employees with that kindness that their property and status in society required of them.[53] Yet the employer, according to Carlyle, confronted by the starving worker, would simply insist that he had paid him to the last sixpence of the agreed terms and that he had nothing further to do with the man's condition.[54] It was the constant theme of these and other social critics, amongst whom Disraeli in particular stands out on this issue, that power and standing within society were legitimate and morally defensible only as long as their possessors accepted obligations and responsibilities as part of their enjoyment of position. The historical validity of these claims is less important than their practical impact on present and future politics.

And drawing together the twin themes of commercialism and irresponsibility was that of individualism, that most highly prized of nineteenth century virtues which the middle classes revelled in and the working classes were perpetually enjoined to acquire. Every man was the maker of his own destiny, and success would come to him who worked industriously and practised virtue: independence and self-help were everything; reliance on others was deplored. It was only the idle and dissatisfied who could be at all alarmed by the Combination Laws, wrote the *Manchester Mercury*, in 1800, for only those who lacked resolution and independence could possibly have the need to act in combination with others.[55] 'Of this bill we can by no means speak favourably', wrote the *Manchester Guardian* of Peter Moore's bill to repeal the Combination Laws and replace them by a whole charter of labour rights in 1823, for such guarantees would give working men such a feather bed to recline upon that they would lose all incentive to individual effort and improvement.[56] Similarly, the House of Commons rejected, in 1821, a notion that they should consider the question of setting up Owenite communities, partly on the grounds that such a system would abolish individuality.[57] The workman must continue to strive on his own and he might thereby, according to an Assistant Commissioner on Handloom Weaving in 1841, raise himself into the ranks of the capitalists.[58] The miners, according to their commissioners in 1844, should abolish all their restrictive practices, for otherwise they would have no chance of saving money and escaping from the mines; it was a curious ideal—career fulfilment that would only be achieved by changing jobs—but such was the hope extended to the brightest aspirants within this occupational group.[59] Encouragement, compulsion even, to pursue individual interest by individual effort had reached a high-point in the new Poor Law of 1834, which treated poverty and unemployment as a personal failure for which the individual must be punished, either by the workhouse, or by removal to some other part of the country if he could not find the means to survive in his own neighbourhood. 'It is a singular pride', wrote Mr Redmond Pilkington of Derby enigmatically in 1834, 'that points to the beauty of its gaols and workhouses; a country might indeed be proud to be without them.'[60] And the country, it could have been argued, might have been without them if all individuals had possessed that virtue and industry that society was now expecting of them. Until they were cured of their various bad habits, members of the working classes could never play their proper role within society, which was that of ambitious and competitive economic man.

But not everyone believed that individualism and the competition of one man against the next were calculated to produce the harmonious society that others thought would result from the pursuit of personal self-interest. This was a society of 'sauve qui peut' and 'the devil take the hindmost', wrote Gravener Henson, the Nottingham trade union leader in 1823, and he wanted nothing of it.[61] 'Yes, my dear children, you must eat each other; we are far too fond parents to interfere with so delightful an amusement.' This, Charles Kingsley's Alton Locke was informed, was the attitude of the government when asked to intervene to suppress cut-throat competition for wages in industry.[62] With the abandonment of all notions of general welfare, according to Oastler, the lucky few prospered at the expense of the degraded many.[63] In Carlyle's view it was the physically strong who survived and were venerated. 'Liberty, I am told, is a divine thing. Liberty when it becomes Liberty to die by starvation is not so divine.'[64] Free competition, Arnold Toynbee was to write many years later, had produced 'wealth without well-being', but successful accumulation was not thought a sufficient justification of the values by which the new society of industrialised Britain was setting such store.[65] A rival or alternative ethic was to be offered, and future generations would find themselves continually having to choose between the two, or between variations of these principal themes to emerge with the Industrial Revolution.

It is perhaps less easy to identify the precise form of this alternative philosophy or ideal than it is to recognise the liberalism of the laissez-faire economists, for doing nothing is a much less controversial approach than doing something, since the something will always be a matter for debate. It can be sought tentatively at first in the conduct of humanitarians, who wanted to humanise and soften the harshness and impersonal rigour of economic laws which were, after all, concerned with the lives of people. They were men of sympathy who wanted to intercede on behalf of the less able, the less successful, those who were not able to exploit the economic opportunities that confronted them during the period of Industrial Revolution. A witness before the Poor Law Commissioners in 1834 questioned the nature of a society where so many people died prematurely through over-eating and over-drinking, whilst some sections of society were denied the very necessities of life.[66] A character in *North and South* asked whether the helpless might not be gently lifted out of the roadway of the conqueror, whom they had no power to join, rather than being left to be trampled underfoot.[67] William Cobbett asked why people could not have some holidays.[68] Dickens looked to personal kindness, sympathy, and under-standing to improve the lot of people, not through social im-provement but through the best elements in human nature.[69] Owen asked that the bodies and minds of workmen should be given as much care and attention as the wood and metals of machinery, for man even as an instrument for the creation of wealth could still be improved as a man.[70] Mr Hardy told Parliament in April 1833, that he would prefer to see the manufactures perish than justice and humanity, while Dr Lyon Playfair, in 1845, reported that 'humanity calls loudly for the interference of a paternal legislature to remedy the evils of the towns'.[71] Even the *Manchester Guardian* came to denounce the growing evil of night and day working and prepared itself for some infringement of sacred economic liberties.[72] All these random points represent a less than systematic approach to the weaknesses and injustices of the economic system, but all at least allow some role for human sympathy and sentiment in the formulation of policy. The social implications of the principles of political economy had left a lot of people unsatisfied that it contained the complete answer to the nation's problems, how-ever much they might have disagreed about that answer.

Human sympathy was at least a start, and the inequalities of the new society were what engaged its attention. Southey showed concern at 'the one who grows rich by the labour of the world', at wealth that flowed in but failed to circulate 'equally and healthfully through the whole system', and the increased numbers and sufferings of the poor, despite growing national wealth.[73] Almost identical was Cobbett's lament that many people should work incessantly to feed those who did not work at all (the idle rich of later days) and the accumulation but not diffusion of wealth.[74] Shelley attacked the unequal distribution of wealth and the social disabilities attendant upon poverty, in particular the duty of the poor, as laid down by Malthus, to stop breeding; he attacked too labour-saving machinery which, he alleged, had failed to lighten the burden of men and instead 'added a weight to the curse imposed on Adam'.[75] Oastler believed also that new machines meant longer hours and worse conditions for the many and luxury for the few, and demanded that no improvements should be adopted without adequate provision being made for those whose labour was being superseded.[76]

These were alleged social injustices—alleged because not all would accept them as fair comment and accurate observation—disabilities deriving from a person's position in society and the free operation of economic laws, which these critics believed could be removed by re-organising society to embody higher ideals of social justice to replace the currently acceptable ideal of the competitive free-for-all. Society should change its order of priorities and start to concern itself with different things; for instance, asked William Thompson in 1827, was the production of cheap cotton cloth more indispensable to human happiness than ensuring that the human race itself should be 'kindly and skilfully nurtured and allowed to increase?'[77]

The alternative ideal was suggested for some by Christianity. J. R. Stephens declared his wish 'to apply God's commandments to the various institutions of the social system', which he believed were currently unable to withstand such a test, whilst Richard Oastler, it has been said, was one of the first men to affirm the relevance of Christianity for an industrial society, and to seek there the moral basis for general principles to govern the operation of an economic system which still functioned apart from any moral considerations.[78] Unlike Robert Owen, in his deep religious conviction and a personal distaste for industrialisation, which he would have stopped had he been able, Oastler shared with Owen the belief that the new economic life was destroying the harmony between men, and that community should replace competition in a country organised for happiness not profit. Moral purpose would replace financial incentive, and this theme, discovered by Cobbett and others in backward looks towards the monastic institutions of the Middle Ages, would be carried forward later by Ruskin and Morris in the nineteenth, and R. H. Tawney in the twentieth century. It was the alternative ethic, the alternative value, but it was not, of course, easy to erect into an alternative social system.

The problem of translating ideas and ideals into social realities is one of politics, and the political debate which the social critics of the 1830s and 1840s conducted, concerned what Parliament could and should do about the problems they had identified and the solutions which they had, however vaguely, begun to outline. Oastler realised the kind of arguments he would have to face when calling for parliamentary action, in particular that interference by the state involved an infringement of liberty, and this argument he rejected on the ground that every law passed by Parliament interfered with somebody's liberty yet laws were necessary for the general good; and it was this general good for which the government was responsible, an invoking of the traditional responsibility for 'commonweal'. It was Britain's social tragedy, said Oastler, that such a system of responsibility and control had been abandoned at the very time it was most needed, that the government was entirely neglecting the principal object for which it existed—the supervision of the wants of the people and the best means of ensuring their comforts and necessities, in particular the contentment and happiness of the labouring classes. The government should once again assume its ancient responsibilities and bring order into this situation of anarchy.[79] This interpretation of the traditional paternalist role of government was supported by Oastler's friend, parson Bull of Bradford, who argued that the existing constitution provided sufficiently for the protection and maintenance of the poor as it was based on the principle that the enfranchised part of the community were bound to take care of the rest, a notion of trusteeship.[80] For Tories such as Oastler and Bull it should have been sufficient for Parliament to be reminded of its obligations for action to ensue; they wanted no reconstitution of Parliament. But they did believe in the need, as William Howitt put it in 1838, for a greater power, the national power, to master the great evil that plagued the country.[81]

This belief did, of course, bring them into direct conflict with those who would have supported Buckle's celebrated dictum that 'Law-givers are nearly always the obstructors of society instead of its helpers', and the laissez-faire extremists who believed that non-interference was just as important a principle for social as for economic policy.[82] But it would be wrong to suppose that a greater role for government had not been foreshadowed in the earlier writings of the political economists, or that the later ones were not drawing some distinction between strictly economic affairs and matters of social administration. Adam Smith had, in the eighteenth century, ascribed to the government the duty to pursue public works which no individual would undertake, in addition to handling defence and justice. In the nineteenth century, both Senior and McCulloch, despite their general stance in opposition to interference, acknowledged that expediency and the general good of the community should determine government, and that laissez-faire should not be applied blindly in all areas, and both accepted the need for government action to deal with many of the problems produced by urbanisation. Absolute positions, in so far as they had ever existed, were clearly collapsing under the pressure of events.[83] In 1834 an Assistant Commissioner on the

Poor Law, D. C. Moylan, confessed that whilst, as a general proposition, he could imagine no greater calamity to the poor themselves than any interference by the legislature in their freedom of labour, yet in the case of children's employment, 'common humanity and the best interests of society' seemed to demand it.[84] These suggested criteria, 'common humanity and the best interests of society', were as much as any of the reformers were attempting to establish and were becoming increasingly acceptable on those questions that were not primarily economic.

The cholera epidemic of 1832 gave impetus to a whole range of enquiries on social questions, and to the growth of a powerful lobby for government action in sanitary reform and education; and in 1840 the Select Committee on the Health of Towns reported its intention to suggest improvements in the towns 'if evils are found to exist there within reach of legislative remedy', and stressed that where problems were not being tackled by local authorities 'it is the duty of the legislature to take efficient steps to protect so numerous and valuable a portion of the community'.[85] Chadwick reported in 1842 that the 'first great remedies' of efficient drainage, sewage, and cleansing of towns had already come 'within the acknowledged province of the legislature', and he went on to list other examples of legislative interference and regulation which 'Public opinion has of late required'. These included the protection of factory children, and the boy chimney-sweeps, rules for the structure of private dwellings to lessen fire hazards, the prevention of overcrowding in private tenements, and the cleansing of metropolitan tenements.[86] These were perhaps less important for the actual substance of their achievement than for the declaration of intent which they involved. It was becoming increasingly realised and accepted that laws and their efficient execution could reduce sickness and disease, and people like Dr Lyon Playfair began to insist that do-gooders should cease to work for ameliorations and be replaced by legislators who could tackle causes.[87]

The horse of freedom, Matthew Arnold was to say, will not

necessarily bring you to the right destination.[88] New destinations were being pointed to and these could only be reached by increasing state intervention; the debate would be on the areas and extent of this intervention, not on the principle of whether it should take place, for laissez-faire or non-intervention by the government in all spheres of national life had never been the practice, and growing intervention would eventually undermine even the theory.

Response on questions of public health and factory reform, and a grudging movement towards the spending of public money on education, first undertaken in 1833, still left untouched the crunch question of whether the power of the capitalist should determine the nature of the new society. 'What we want principally', said Oastler, 'is to cut the dreadful power of capital', for it was the growth and concentration of capital, he believed, that were destroying the old routines of work and life, and injecting the alien morality of competition; the teachings of the economists could not be reconciled with the gospel of fellowship, and capitalism must be eliminated, or at least controlled, if fellowship were to triumph. He thought regulation and protection might come in the form of his proposed regional tribunals, which would fix minimum wages, maximum hours, and the general conditions of industry; in this way the fangs of capitalism might be drawn, even if the institution itself did not disappear.[89]

In 1835, the handloom weavers received a surprisingly sympathetic hearing from a committee of enquiry whose report, though ultimately disregarded, gave them some grounds for supposing that Parliament might be willing to intervene on their behalf over wages and machinery and break those sacred economic laws that had previously been considered inviolable. The laws remained safe, though they had at least been brought into serious question, and the House of Commons was clearly not ready for so radical a departure in Oastler's direction. For Owen, the answer would be in co-operative communities, where common welfare and moral regulation would replace

114

private profit as the aim of industrial production. Owen's solution required a massive act of consent from the working classes to the benevolent, paternalistic design that he had worked out for them, a design which envisaged no political role for the workers in the achievement or running of their new world. Oastler at least looked to Parliament to accomplish the changes he envisaged, and when he saw that a Parliament elected on a middle-class franchise would not bring about the changes he wanted, he became, along with Stephens, a reluctant democrat, involving himself, with reservations, in the campaigns of Chartism. Parson Bull had warned the Poor Law Commissioners that if Parliament, as then constituted, did not look after the working classes, they would soon wish to look after themselves, and he was no lover of democracy either.[90]

If looking after the working classes involved intervention in the economy, then such a thing remained a very distant prospect, for the very men who contributed most memorably on the social questions, like Chadwick or Macaulay, went out of their way to reaffirm their continued adherence to laissez-faire principles on economic affairs, and the Benthamites who contributed to the growth of government in certain spheres, continued to oppose its extension to others.[91] Yet the serious dilemma seen by Oastler and his contemporaries produced no radical solution. The capitalist society had come to stay, and the powers of the capitalist, in so far as they were successfully challenged, were eroded very gradually by piecemeal legislation and the rival institutions that the working classes were able eventually to mobilise against them, and even these served to confirm the existence of capitalism rather than to destroy it. Such has been the British capacity to adapt rather than revolutionise, that even the alternative ideal of co-operation, which was ranged against competition in the early nineteenth century, now seems to many of its advocates attainable through a modified and civilised capitalism.

Notes to this chapter are on page 180.

5 The Search for the Past

A social revolution as dramatic and fundamental as that which accompanied the Industrial Revolution in Great Britain, could not have taken place without some members experiencing an acute sense of loss. Rapid change, which permitted within one person's lifetime a comparison between different ways of life, must inevitably have prompted the feeling in many that all change was not necessarily for the good, and that what had been left behind was in many ways preferable to that which was now being experienced. Without question, the experiences of many first and second generation industrial workers were harsh in the extreme, and it is not surprising that the view developed that the misfortunes of the working classes could be traced to the process of industrialisation, even if the concept was not yet clearly formalised. A corollary of this view, the belief that pre-industrial society was more just and happy, is also to be found, and depended to some extent on memories of distant childhood or beliefs about times not actually experienced. Whatever the factual basis on which it was constructed, a theme of nostalgia for times past is to be found throughout the decades of greatest industrial change and persists beyond them. Over a longer period, the Industrial Revolution, like the Norman Conquest, would help to create the myth of a preceding 'golden age'.

It is common to exaggerate both the speed of social change and the individual's sense of perspective on the events through which he is living, and to forget that a man is always living in what is for him the present day. Reflections and recollections of earlier times are not as commonly encountered as some have supposed, and it is very clear that the majority who lived through the Industrial Revolution did not spend their time bemoaning the processes of change which they were experiencing. Some, nevertheless, did attempt to cling to a passing world whose virtues they appreciated and whose passage they only suspected. In 1804, for instance, William Wilberforce, though willing to lift the paternalistic restrictions earlier imposed upon the clothing trade, stated that 'he would never consent to any measure that might alter or interrupt that general system of domestic industry and domestic happiness which prevailed among the cloth manufacturers of the county he had the honour to represent.'[1] He liked the domestic structure of the clothing trade, so attractively described by the Committee on the State of Woollen Manufactures in 1806, and so too did James Graham, a member of the committee, who maintained that, 'If the factory system were to exclude from the country the domestic system it would be dreadful indeed, for it is very pleasing in Yorkshire to see the domestic clothiers living in a field,' with their homesteads, rather than shut up in a street.' His interest, he said, in the success of the factory system was as nothing compared with the interest he had in the preservation and prosperity of the domestic system. And he was supported in these sentiments by Walter Spencer Stanhope of Horsforth, who had no apprehensions that factories were on the increase and would have acted otherwise, he said, had he thought otherwise.[2]

Their faith was a touching testimony to the excellent qualities of a system that was about to disappear. So too was Mr Baring's admission, in March 1817, that 'he should have wished that a great deal of this machinery never had existence', for 'he would have certainly preferred to see each cottage door with its spinning wheel as was formerly the case'.[3] Even more innocent was the belief of Mr Stuart Wortley, in December 1819, that in the agricultural counties 'the peasant looked up to the farmer, the farmer to his landlord, the proprietor to the peer, and the peer to the Crown, thus forming a connected chain which bound the highest and lowest classes of society together', a situation quite different from that which prevailed in the manufacturing districts.[4] Parliament seems to have been almost the best place to look for mistaken notions about the nature of the society that it had pretensions to govern.

One element of continuity between pre-industrial society and that of the early nineteenth century, which seems to have delighted observers wherever they found it, was the ability of some industrial workers to return to agricultural work at certain times of the year, delaying a little longer that specialised or differentiated role that modern society had in store for them. Enquiries into the condition of the handloom weavers in 1839, revealed that the Scottish weavers around Largs derived a small income from fishing and letting out boats in the season, but this was admitted to be exceptional. In the south-west of England, weavers could occasionally get other kinds of work, but again this was admitted to be exceptional and confined to large agricultural districts where specialised divisions of labour had not yet fully taken place. Around Leeds it was alleged that the Bramley weavers still went hay-making, though a Pudsey witness denied that there were other opportunities in the area and said that when trade failed there was nothing to which the weavers could turn.[5] There were similar contradictions and ambiguities in the evidence given to the Framework-knitters' Commission of 1845 about the extent to which the stockingers of the East Midlands had kept up their gardens or tended allotments and the availability of harvesting as an alternative employment in the appropriate season.[6] From Renfrew in Scotland, the *New Statistical Account* reported in 1845 on the beneficial effects of seasonal employment in the fields, a practice said to be common amongst the womenfolk, of whom a considerable number put aside their 'needles and other implements of manufacture' in the summer and the autumn, 'and hire themselves to the farmers in the neighbourhood at potato-planting, hay-making, hoeing and weeding, and latterly, at reaping, digging potatos, and raising turnips.'[7]

It is impossible to measure accurately the extent to which

118

large numbers of industrial workers retained this 'mixed economy'; nor is it possible to say whether those who did so were consciously seeking to preserve an old way of life, or were simply desperate to eke out a precarious existence by whatever means could be found. The trend was certainly towards differentiation of roles. The Spitalfields silk weavers would have been too preoccupied with the struggle for survival after the first quarter of the nineteenth century to contribute much to the scientific and rural pursuits for which they had been famed earlier, and Mrs Gaskell's Job Legh, whose study of living creatures and amateur scientific work is thought to make him a representative figure, was an old man and presumably no longer working; as a factory worker or a handloom weaver he would scarcely have had much time to devote to his pursuit.[8] It would always be interesting for town-dwellers to hear that a hive of bees at Flixton had produced seventy-four pounds of honey or that a good harvest was in prospect, but when Cobbett, on his way through Worcester, recorded that a good large garden and pig-stys were 'the only security for happiness in a labourer's family, whatever the feelosophers say', it was not the industrial worker he had in mind.[9] Similarly, his remark of 14 September 1816, that if Mr Gray had sown his mangle-wurzle seed in firmly broken ground his crops would never have failed, was addressed to countrymen and not to the urban workers who were now reading him in such numbers.[10]

It might be argued that the domestic worker of the manufacturing trades remained, throughout the first half of the nineteenth century, a countryman at heart, for it was the domestic worker who was most given to reminiscence about former times. The cotton spinners are supposed to have regarded the decade 1780–90 as their 'golden age', in that they enjoyed the increased earnings that the jenny made possible, without having to endure the factory that the water-frame and the mule made necessary. But the spinners were to remain largely silent about their memories, and it might be said that the factory workers as a whole were not inclined to reminisce about the delights of pre-factory times.[11] This must cast some doubt on those interpretations of working-class political protest which identify hostility to industrialisation as a prime grievance; the factory workers tended to be well behaved except in times of severe depression, and it was left largely to the outworkers to stage whatever protest was mobilised. It was the outworkers who were the great ones for remembering the past, in part, presumably, because they were the ones who suffered most by industrialisation and had most cause to remember with fondness what they had lost.

Of the domestic workers, the weavers had the richest memories, as they testified before a select committee in 1834. One Scot, comparing his diet and style of living with that of forty years earlier, recalled that 'in former times . . . the weaver could sit down to a tea-breakfast and have his butter and ham like an ordinary furnished table; but the general breakfast now is porridge and buttermilk, and the dinner, potatoes and possibly a herring, or any cheap article; as for broth and flesh meat, it is a very rare thing that it is in a weaver's house.' Forty years earlier, he said, it had been common to buy a small cow to salt up for winter. Another, James Orr of Paisley, recalled his youth when 'it was quite common for a handloom-weaver to lay in as much meat, potatoes, cheese and butter in harvest as would serve till spring, and coals were laid in in larger quantities, and very commonly handloom-weavers salted meat at Martinmas for winter; now it requires the clubbing of all the little earnings of the family on Saturday to make provision for the ensuing week'. 'I do not think', said another weaver, 'that commerce which renders the people more distressed is a desirable thing at all.' Certainly the weavers remained very conscious of the changes in their own prosperity since 1800, and agreed in their recollections of the 'good old times', 'when their labours were four-fold re-numerated'. And it would be difficult to dispute the accuracy of their recollections.[12] Similarly with the stocking knitters, whose nineteenth century memories of more affluent times, if a little exaggerated, were prompted by recalling pre-war wages of up to 30/- (£1.50) per week for the skilled man, and 10–12/- (50–60p) for the least skilled, which contrasted very favourably with Felkin's estimate of an average wage of 6/- (30p) per week over the period 1815–50.[13] Also featuring in the memories were the pig or the cow that each stockinger was said to have, plus the garden and the home-grown vegetables. These must have virtually disappeared shortly after 1800; the poverty of the country-dwellers and the housing of the town-dwellers precluded these amenities.

A preference for the countryside rather than the town seems to have played no very strong part in the tradition of the urban worker. Against Dodd's doubtfully reliable narrative entitled *The Factory System Illustrated*, in which there appears a not altogether convincing mother of crippled children who recalls her life in the country and the almost inevitable cow that belonged to the family, can be balanced Cooke Taylor's Lancashire operatives who told him that however severe industrial depression might become, they dreaded nothing more than being forced to return to the farm.[14] Thomas Hood's workman with needle and thread who expressed the longing,

> Oh! but to breathe the breath
> Of the cowslip and primrose sweet—
> With the sky above my head,
> And the grass beneath my feet,
> For only one short hour
> To feel as I used to feel,
> Before I knew the woes of want
> And the walk that costs a meal!

was expressing a preference for leisure and affluence over toil and poverty, and a liking for the countryside, and it would be an exaggeration to see this as an indictment of the Industrial Revolution. Too much could similarly be made of Martha's perfectly understandable preference for Fieldhead Hollow before the mill came, at the end of *Shirley*: 'Different to what it is now. . . . A lonesome spot it was—and a bonnie spot—full of oak trees and nut trees. It is altered now.'[15] And it is again altered, though there are still plenty of oak trees and nut trees as well as two motorways close to the site of Charlotte Brontë's Hollow's Mill.

The old land did not, in fact, disappear as speedily and comprehensively as its doughtiest champions seemed to be implying, and the contemporary tributes to its beauties and virtues which industrialisation prompted, are paradoxically both an idealisation of its qualities and an underestimate of the extent to which its essential nature was being preserved. Dodd's trite description of 'the cheering influences of the sun, the refreshing breeze, the singing of birds', for example, lists amenities which are still universally available, providing the sun shines, and the Industrial Revolution scarcely affected the frequency of this phenomenon.[16] In 1792 the Hon John Byng, appalled by the 'hourly-increasing Birmingham' and the evidence he encountered of depopulation as a result of enclosure, proscribed mud dwellings for his own tenants and prescribed that his 'comfortable cottagers shall be obliged to have land, and to be happy'; fed on a diet of potatoes and buttermilk (hardly the most exotic fare) their children would always compare favourably with those 'fed with hot, black tea'.[17] Byng's prejudices on tea were shared by Cobbett, who had a similar capacity for making the most of a patch of countryside untouched by enclosure or industry. 'All around this great tract of land', he wrote in July 1813, 'which is called waste, the borders are studded with cottages of various dimensions and forms, but the more beautiful for this diversity. . . . These wastes, as they are called, are the blessing and ornament of this part of the kingdom.'[18]

William Howitt, specifically in search of 'the rural life of England' in 1838, discovered 'delicious cottages and gardens, the open common . . . the scores of sweet old-fashioned hamlets, where an humble sociality and primitive simplicity yet remain . . . villagers . . . the old, in their last tranquil days, seated in their easy chairs, or on the stone bench at their doors, glad to chat with you . . . nowhere affluence, but everywhere plenty and comfort observable.' He extolled the advantages of the rural population, 'a taste for the enjoyment of nature . . . the pleasantness of their quiet lives and of their cottages and gardens . . . the freshness of the air and country around them, especially as contrasted with the poor and squalid alleys where those of their own rank, living in towns, necessarily take up their abode . . . the advantages in point of health and purity afforded to their children by their position.' The world had no more beautiful sight, he wrote, 'than that of our English cottages, in those parts of the country where the violent changes of the times have not been so sensibly felt.' 'Blessings be on them wherever they stand, in woodland valleys, or on open heaths, throughout fair England.' Alas, poor Lancashire no longer contained these delights, 'picturesque villages and cottages half buried in their garden and orchard trees; no longer those home-crofts, with their old, tall hedges; no longer rows of bee-hives beneath their little thatched southern sheds; those rich fields and farm houses, surrounded with wealth of corn-ricks, and herds and flocks. You have no longer that quiet and Arcadian-looking population.'[19] This was now a land of Industrial Revolution, of North and South. And if this was an overdrawn picture in terms of the old countryside, the same could hardly be said of Pugin's description of the medieval towns, which he contrasted not at all unreasonably with the ugly creations of the industrial age.[20]

A matter of far greater interest and concern than the old land was the old society that inhabited it. But not only was the old society more interesting; it was also more elusive and has continued so, for the land at least has remained and left more clues behind about its earlier state. If Robert Owen is to be believed, the old aristocracy of birth 'were in many respects superior to the money-making and money-seeking aristocracy of modern times', and informed by their example and under their kindly supervision, 'the lower orders experienced not only a considerable degree of comfort but frequent opportunities of enjoying healthy rational sports and amusements.'[21] Howitt hoped to recapture these days so that England could again have 'humble homesteads, where a father and his sons may work together . . . where a lowly, but a happy people may congregate at Xmas and other festivals', people whom Coleridge saw as 'a healthful, callous-handed, but high and warmhearted tenantry . . . ready to march off at the first call' to their country's defence.[22] One of Disraeli's characters in *Sybil* looked back for his comparisons to the days before the Wars of the Roses, when the people were allegedly better fed, clothed, and lodged than in the 1830s, whilst another wished for the return of the days of Richard I, though his friend grimly suggested that this would mean a return of serfdom.[23] Cobbett looked back rather more vaguely to an unspecified time in the past when there were no paupers and no poor rates, 'when labouring men were clothed in good woollen cloth' and all had plenty of meat and bread and beer; this they would have enjoyed amidst the 'plain manners and plentiful living' of such a place as Charrington's farm, Reigate, where Cobbett attended a sale on 20 October 1825, and noted the 'oak clothes-chests, oak bedsteads, oak chests of drawers, and oak tables to eat on, long, strong, and well supplied with joint stools', all the furniture, like the people, plain, strong and reliable. Such sound, commendable, and functional people Cobbett identified in his own time amongst the coal-diggers, iron-smelters, and knife-makers; although they lived away from the land, which was the source of most of the virtues which he admired, he admitted that society should supply these groups with food 'very cheerfully in exchange for the produce of their rocks and the wondrous works of their hands'.[24] Although the composite picture of pre-industrial man is built up from a variety of imaginations, ranging over a variety of centuries, he emerges clearly enough as a plain, simple, humble, reliable, contented being who wanted for nothing in the unsophisticated yet totally satisfying society of which he was part. Industrial man by implication, and often by explicit denial, had lost all these qualities of excellence, and the sophisticated society to which he belonged was totally unsatisfying.

The nature of pre-industrial society is even more elusive, perhaps because less concrete, than the nature of man within it. Frequently nineteenth century social critics looked to the medieval monastery as their social ideal, and then slipped into a vague assumption that the values of pre-industrial society were somehow embodied in this ideal. Carlyle's description of Abbot Samson and his monastic community has been seen as the most substantial and literal vision of the medieval order seen by the social critics, but others followed the same line of thought.[25] Southey praised the social role of monasteries, Pugin commended their role in the local community and the characteristically kindly master and well-fed, well-clothed poor in their care, and even the earthly Cobbett saw them as an ideal social institution. Disraeli's Sybil desired as her fondest wish 'to see the people once more kneel before our blessed Lady', when all would once again, presumably, become part of the integrated society and be cared for as those for whom the monasteries had cared.[26]

Why the nineteenth-century writers should have needed to go back as far as pre-Reformation times to find their point of comparison is not clear. It is probably true that it was easier to reach agreement about the fourteenth century than something so recent as eighteenth-century society, though ease of agreement by no means ensured accuracy of account. Also, the monastery was the best available image of what they had in mind, and if that particular institution had ceased to function with the Reformation, society had, up to the Industrial Revolution, continued, it was believed, to embody many of its principles, though some had been neglected or fallen into disuse. Lord Henry, of Coningsby's acquaintance, 'represented to the duke that the order of the peasantry was as ancient, legal, and recognised an order as the order of the nobility . . .

that the parochial constitution of this country was more important than its political constitution . . .'; the order of the peasantry must be restored to its former condition 'not merely in physical comfort . . . but to its condition in all those moral attributes which make a recognised rank in a nation.'[27] In the past, argued Robert Owen, the poor had been trained by the example of some landed proprietor and, fortified by this example and protection, had themselves been members of respectable family units.[28] This integration, this social relationship of interdependence amongst gentry, squirearchy, the farmers, and their labourers, had been the character of society as long as land had been the basis of life and wealth, and had persisted until the corrupting influence of commerce, finance, and industry had crept in. The new economic system and the new values which it spawned had destroyed these bonds between men; the reverence and affection, said Oastler, which workmen had felt towards their employers when he was young were gone.[29] New times had brought new ways.

In particular they had brought the factory system, and no aspect of the disappearing society was to receive more attention than the domestic system of production, even though its disappearance was neither so speedy nor so complete as many supposed it to be. Where it persisted in large industries, such as cotton weaving, the weaving of wool, and stocking knitting, it did, however, acquire the characteristics of 'sweated' trade and so encouraged the contemporary fondness for enthusiastic accounts of what it had been like before the great changes. 'Or iver you set up the pole o' your tent amang us, Mr Moore', said Brontë's Moses Barraclough to the mill-owner, 'we lived i' peace and quietness; yea, I may say, in all loving-kindness.' These were the days 'when hand-labours were encouraged and respected, and no mischief-maker had ventured to introduce these here machines, which is so pernicious.'[30] The peace, the quiet, and the loving-kindness are important, for they repeatedly featured in the traditional accounts of that way of life, and even in the 1880s Arnold Toynbee, who recognised the existence of brutal and ignorant masters, quoted twice over with evident approval, an earlier sentiment that masters and men had been so joined together in love in the domestic system that they did not wish to be separated.[31] Cobbett for his part, liked the domestic system because it kept people on the land; he reported with pleasure from Ryall in Worcestershire, in 1826, that glove-manufacturing, which he believed, mistakenly, could not be carried on by machinery, was keeping the working people prosperous. It was done by the women and children in the cottages, whilst their menfolk worked in the fields and hop-gardens, 'to raise the food and the drink and the wool. This is a great thing for the land.' Without the domestic industry poor folk would be thrown on the parish and eventually driven to the towns.[32] He developed the same theme in the *Political Register*. Describing his boyhood memories he recalled that:

> In those 'dark ages' the farmers' wives and daughters and servant maids were spinning, reeling, carding, knitting, or at something or other of that sort, whenever the work of the farm-house did not demand them.
> The manufacturing which was thus divided amongst the millions of labourers' wives and children, while it was a great blessing to the labouring people themselves, was also a great benefit to the landowner.

It kept people on the land and allowed agriculture to prosper.[33]

Cobbett was not just talking about economic viability, but of a whole way of life, a quality of existence, a system of values almost. The same thing is evident in S. H. Kydd's *History of the Factory Movement*, written in 1857. Here he describes the delights of domestic manufacture, the pleasant whirring of the spinning-wheel which permitted conversation to take place, the good health that this employment sustained, the promotion of parental authority and filial obedience that was engendered, and 'the growth of domestic sympathies'.[34] This is also true of

Peter Gaskell's almost classic idealisation of domestic industry in 1836, a system which produced 'golden times' for the labourer; he was a respectable man of moral worth, simple habits, and few wants, producing enough to feed and clothe his family, to which he was a good son, a good husband, or a good father as his role evolved. He worked hard when necessity demanded, and his vacant hours he occupied in farming the few acres that he rented, which were a valuable part of his domestic economy.[35] It is the integrity of the people, and the moral worth of the system that shine through these accounts, and warnings have been given that the men themselves, as opposed to their literary patrons, can be found defending actually existing social relationships rather than looking back to mythical 'golden ages' as some of their champions were inclined to do.[36] Such men gave evidence in 1803 and 1806 against the growth of factories in the woollen trade.[37] Of course, Gaskell's domestic worker is too good to be true, and other contemporaries such as Andrew Ure did a heavy debunking exercise by exposing 'the abject condition of so-called independent handicraft labourers' in the 1830s.[38] This has remained a favourite sport amongst historians too. For example, the absence of 'rural innocence and happiness to the north of Coventry' in the early nineteenth century has been used to prevent any romantic contrasts being drawn between the domestic and the urban factory workers in the ribbon-trade.[39]

The reality and detailed accuracy of this social ideal developed by critics of early nineteenth-century society are not supportable propositions. It can readily be seen to be an agglomeration of bits and pieces from many centuries; it is never quite clear if it is intended as an historical account of an actual period of time and, if so, exactly which period is under consideration. It is a mixture of some ideas that could fairly be assumed to belong to certain times past, others that are little short of romance, and others that represent future aspirations rather than any past achievements. The accuracy of the picture is of secondary importance; a few incisive stabs can quickly fill it with holes. Even Disraeli's own descriptions of the similar predicament of the industrial and rural poor undermines any tendency to romanticise the agricultural society that might be encouraged by Mrs Gaskell's *North and South*.[40] It is a mistaken view of the eighteenth century, says one historian, that 'custom was the shield of the poor'; this old social order, says another, was hard, brutal, and exploitative, neither moral nor natural, where property was held in men as well as in land, and infringements of property rights were met by a grim and savage penal system.[41] The realism of the latter is clearly more convincing than the idealism of the former account, yet ideas can be just as important as facts, and wrong ideas just as powerful as right ones. The critics had a standard and an ideal, however derived, and the deficiencies which these measures seemed to reveal were an incentive to political action and so were important. The old system was seen to be collapsing, even if it had never existed; the labourer was still as willing to work and as anxious to please as he ever was, the Poor Law Commissioners were told, but the warm and fervent feeling towards his employers was no longer there.[42] Political economy had triumphed, said Michael Sadler in 1831, and the old society had gone with it; there was no room for the little cultivator, for the poor, for their gardens, and their cows, and the best of the cottages were already demolished.[43]

Some sense and awareness that times were changing prompted responses that were many and varied, and even within individuals as confused as the notions that inspired them. Cobbett, it has been said, attempted to salvage what he could of the old way of life in his *Cottage Economy*, collecting and publishing what he could as a guide to country living, for example how to make bread or how to look after animals.[44] He appeared at times to be looking towards parliamentary reform, of all things, to stop the developments he deplored and restore society to its former state; yet at other times he seems to have decided that any hope for the future must lie with the industrial working classes and not with the farmers, and he increasingly became their spokesman, thereby committing himself to improving the future rather than reconstructing the past. Oastler had similar problems. He hated industrialism and a society which could pass the Poor Law of 1834, and he took as his motto 'The Altar, the Throne, and the Cottage'. Yet even with this backward look he was one of the first popular leaders to utilise modern political techniques to accomplish the social reform that would make industrialism more tolerable, thereby contributing considerably to its survival, and his Tory democracy was as democratic as it was Tory. Robert Owen, with his own mixture of contradictions, was no democrat for all his associations with socialism; his methods were of the past, and he assigned no political role to working men, despite his personal career as an industrialist and his philanthropic intention that modern industrial power should be made to work for the community as a whole. The community, whether at New Lanark or in a village of co-operation, was the hierarchical, paternalistic society of the past, with Robert Owen himself the great father-figure. And a later escapist rebel from industrialism, William Morris, who hated the factories and the towns, and who created his imaginary 'Nowhere' without them and without their morality, saw at the same time that industrialisation, which created the working class, might give that body a power to transform the society which had created it. Plotting a course for the future was then no easier than determining the course of the past.

And before the future could be realistically faced there had to be overcome what might be termed the psychological barrier associated with the role of the land in national life and the national economy, and the inability or reluctance to admit that its status was changing for all time as Britain became an industrial economy and the majority of its people became separated from the land. For a long time people persisted in the belief that the solutions to the problems of an industrial society were to be found on the land, and for as long, genuine solutions escaped them. It seemed so obvious to Gaskell, for instance, that a country which suffered from periodic unemployment and imported a growing proportion of its food, should look for a solution to both problems in the cultivation of its waste lands. About sixteen million acres, he believed, were capable of being so utilised for the performance of this great remedial work within society.[45] This would have required enterprise and organisation on an enormous scale, and Richard Oastler for one believed that the government ought to take the lead in promoting land-resettlement and the establishment of peasant smallholdings. Every cottage, he urged, should be given a small plot of land to enable the farm-labourer to have a greater stake in the country than his present one, and great benefits would ensue, to the individual and to the nation, from this broadly-based system of peasant proprietors. In addition, the state should sponsor the reclamation of wastes, and drained lands could be leased to the unemployed, a more humane and attractive policy than fostering emigration, which he sternly opposed.[46] Although William Cobbett was very free with his advice to those contemplating emigration as an answer to their problems, he too, of course, was anxious to develop the land as much as possible, and urged, in 1811, 'the adoption of such measures as would give all possible facility to the employment of additional hands in agriculture'.[47] This course of action still seemed very attractive to witnesses before the Poor Law Commissioners in the 1830s. One informed the commissioners that the country contained not one labourer more than could be profitably employed upon the land, and the answer was to give the poor half an acre at their own door at a fair rent to keep them at work. J. C. Blackden of Northumberland proposed the revival of Tudor legislation, repealed in the eighteenth century, which rendered it obligatory upon landowners to attach at least four acres of land to each cottage built upon their property.[48] And these proposals were paralleled by innumerable allotment schemes which were undertaken throughout the country, in part to relieve poverty, in part to attempt to recreate the ideal, self-sufficient subsistence worker, who need not depend for his survival on the vagaries of trade, but who could always turn for relief to his own horticultural efforts. The idea has remained a very attractive one.

These schemes would supplement industry, but other, more drastic ideas, involved a complete rejection of the whole process of industrialisation, or at least a complete rejection of industrial society. Robert Owen's co-operative communities were to accept industry and redeploy it for communal advantage, to be microcosms of the national economy without the ideology that inspired it, and to devote themselves to moral regeneration. The early co-operative societies of the 1820s and 1830s hoped to raise money to establish small communities which would eliminate all the ills and evils that the larger society was now breeding, and not until 1860 did shop-keeping replace community building as their avowed aim.[49] They in turn inspired a variety of other societies with similar aims; the National Community Friendly Society of Salford, 1837, which planned to use its funds 'First, for the purchase or rental of land to erect suitable dwellings and other buildings . . .'; the Redemption Societies such as that at Leeds, founded in 1845, which ran for some years a community settlement in Wales, or the Bury Redemption Society which planned 'To purchase and cultivate land upon the co-operative principle'.[50] Although these various groups had the appearance of wishing to opt out of society, they regarded their efforts as positive and constructive attempts to remodel society by showing how its advances could best be put to the advantage of the population as a whole, a not unworthy purpose.

The most famous of all the settlement schemes, the Chartist Land Co-operative Society of 1845—later renamed the National Land Company—was Fergus O'Connor's plan. It was not only a scheme which opted out of society but it was consciously backward-looking. Like all the other schemes, it owed a great deal to the Owenite communities, but its distinct tone was set by the proposal to establish members of the working classes in villages as peasant proprietors. They were to rent their own separate holdings and to own what they produced; the scheme was a hybrid involving individualism on the one hand but without the industrial development that was making the principle profitable in the world outside. It was a deliberate turning back of the clock, and its capacity to attract to visions of a rural life so many of the industrial working classes, initially from the factory districts but later from a wide variety of areas, suggests a fairly substantial element was as yet unappeased by the way of life and material benefits that industrialisation was offering. Some 70,000 people subscribed £100,000 to the Land Scheme, but a mere 250 actually reached land, the first ones at O'Connorville near Rickmansworth, and the project collapsed with some acrimony.[51]

Disraeli's characters, Lord Everingham and Lord Henry and their followers in real life, would continue to argue on the one hand that dancing round maypoles did the poor no good, on the other that it did them no harm, but this, to say the least, was a peripheral issue.[52] And peripheral too was the contribution to the solution of society's problems by those people who continued to find a way out of the world by creating their model communities with varying degrees of rural innocence.

Notes to this chapter are on page 183.

6 Reform and Reconciliation

It has already been suggested that the most remarkable thing about the far-reaching economic and social changes known as the Industrial Revolution was the fact that they occurred without any accompanying political revolution. There were, of course, several minor abortive insurrectionary attempts within the period spanned by Europe's two great years of revolution, 1789 and 1848, but these made little impact upon the political system, which was able to adjust itself gradually and peacefully to accommodate the new social forces that were exerting pressure. The establishment faced a two-fold threat, from the manufacturing interest—the middle-class threat—and from the working classes, and it was the successful containment of these two hazards that constituted its great political achievement in the nineteenth century. And this act of containment was at the same time the process by which industrialisation became the settled and accepted way of life for most of the British people.

The first threat, from the manufacturers, was more apparent than real; the violent rhetoric with which the landed interest was lambasted over the issues of parliamentary reform and the repeal of the Corn Laws, and the repeated emphasis of the supposedly conflicting interests of the parties involved, can not detract from the traditional involvement of many landed families in commercial and industrial enterprises long before this time. There had never been the distaste for or prohibition of commercial enterprise in Britain that had helped to give the French aristocracy, for instance, a purely ornamental role in times past, and landed families had for centuries improved their fortunes and their bloodstock by intermarriage with those families whose fortunes were not of landed origin. The ability of wealth to break down social barriers, the willingness of aristocratic patrons to take an interest in early industrial enterprise, and the role of many landed families as agricultural innovators and agrarian capitalists in the eighteenth century, all helped to create a climate of opinion in which industrial change could go ahead without any serious risk of severe alienation of the aristocracy. Parliamentary debates of the late eighteenth century suggest a universal welcome for the new vitality of the economy and the impetus that was being derived from the establishment and swift expansion of the cotton trade.

The classic entrepreneurial figures of the Industrial Revolution—Strutt, Arkwright, or Robert Peel—were all self-made men of modest origin, but this should not distract attention from the role of landowners in industrial development, which has been suggested as having a significance equal to the part they played in agricultural development over the long period, 1700–1870.[1] The largest of them all, the 1st Duke of Sutherland, was it has been argued, 'the most remarkable demonstration of the use of an aristocratic fortune in an age of revolution', and his family fortunes derived mainly from his participation in the industrial development of the economy, with substantial interests in canals, railways, and mines, allowed him to re-invest industrial profits in largely abortive attempts to stimulate the crofter economy of rural Sutherland.[2] The Duke of Devonshire was said to derive an annual income of £12,000–15,000 from lead-mining in the middle years of the nineteenth century, whilst the list of Northumberland and Durham colliery owners was 'nearly a handbook of the nobility and gentry of these counties'. Many families, by sitting still and doing nothing, could enjoy greatly enhanced incomes from urban rents and mineral royalties as land values increased and the minerals became so much in demand. Others took an active promoting interest in the history of turnpike roads, making rivers navigable, the building of canals and harbours, the establishment of banks, and the building of towns.[3] Despite the individual antipathies of particular landowners to specific projects, an unsightly mine, a new road, or an industrial town that might destroy the amenity of a family seat, it would be quite impossible to argue that the landed interest as a whole set its face against industrialisation and had to be coerced by a hated middle class and made to give up a rural economy for an industrial one which it resisted bitterly.

This was not the way of industrial change in Great Britain, and if the economic revolution was accomplished without sharp social cleavage between land and industry, there is less reason to suppose that the political change which it required was of necessity radical and vehemently contested. It has been argued on the one hand that the landed aristocracy paid a heavy price in the long-run for their ability to supplement their wealth from non-agricultural means, that their social ascendancy was diminished and their political ascendancy destroyed, though the process was admittedly a slow one of 'almost imperceptible erosion'.[4] Against this it has been maintained that the aristocracy and gentry were little affected by industrialisation, and even then for the better; with all their economic gains they retained their social predominance and local political power, and their national power too was hardly weakened.[5] The problem is in part one of fixing a time-scale. Liberal governments at the end of the nineteenth century were just as aristocratic as Tory ones at the beginning of that century, but Tory ones were much less so three quarters of the way through the next. The power has been dispersed, but so slowly, and leaving behind so many residual advantages, that the nineteenth-century act of self-preservation might indeed be regarded as a great success. Peel, it has been said, not only saved the aristocracy by repealing the Corn Laws in 1846, thereby removing the poison from the body politic, but he also did this by deliberate intent, in the same way that Lords Grey and Russell, fourteen years earlier, had persuaded a landed

Parliament to accept a conservative measure of parliamentary reform that would, by broadening the power basis a little, leave the essential structure and its own interests substantially intact. And Peel was able to do this because the landed aristocracy were not committed irrevocably to agriculture and against industry; their interests were nicely diversified and nicely balanced and their fortunes were by no means totally dependent on the prosperity of their corn-growing tenant farmers.[6] The aristocracy were not so much defeated in 1846, as persuaded to take the logical step that followed from the 1832 Reform Act, when they had opened their ranks a little to increase the size of the governing establishment. In parliamentary terms the Peelites, very appropriately, were the businessmen who were assimilated into the landed oligarchy.[7] The marriage of Sybil to Lord Evremont was not so much the symbolic fulfilment of Disraeli's wish to see the people united with an enlightened aristocracy, as, in consequence of Sybil's revealed identity, the joining together of the landed interest with the industrial, from which it had, of course, never been truly separated.[8]

The other threat, from the working classes, was potentially much more serious, and did not seem as easily open to solution by slight political manipulation as that from the manufacturers. For the working classes were the makers, not the possessors, of wealth, and could not be admitted into the political establishment with any assurance that their grievances were moderate and easily accommodated. With Cobbett arguing that society was 'daily advancing to the state in which there are but two classes of men, masters and abject dependants', demanding that the working classes should recognise their position, and expressing the belief that change for the better could come only from working people; and with Carlyle admitting that the condition of the English working people was so wrong that they ought not to rest quietly under it; and with fear of working-class revolt almost universal amongst the possessing classes, the scene appeared to be set for major social upheaval.[9] Through the social novels of Disraeli, Gaskell, Dickens, Elliot, and Kingsley, the theme of the dreaded working-class violence runs strongly, and all the writers, however sensitive their appreciation of the working-class predicament, joined together to urge, vainly as they probably imagined, the workers to desist from politics, which they equated with violence, and put their trust elsewhere, in the aristocracy, human nature, or God himself.

In fact, working-class violence played only a minor part in working-class response, and the whole 'working class revolt against the misery and humiliation brought about by the Industrial Revolution', in Beatrice Webb's rather disparaging words, 'had its fling in the twenties and thirties and its apotheosis in the Chartist Movement of the forties.'[10] Whether a self-conscious working class did or did not emerge during the early decades of the nineteenth century, the working-class revolution was certainly a non-event, and the reasons for this might well throw some light on the whole working-class concept. Engels was probably right to argue that the Industrial Revolution forced the workers to think and demand for themselves a position worthy of men, and Beatrice Webb had some justification for her belief that since the oppression and fraudulence of the industrial system forced men to co-operate in pursuit of representative institutions, it could be argued that they served some useful purpose.[11] Yet 'the civilising force of a new vision of society' embodying 'the hopes of generations of the oppressed and exploited' was not felt until the end of the nineteenth and beginning of the twentieth century.[12] In the short run, the workers proved not much more difficult to assimilate than their employers.

The principal means towards reconciliation was the adoption of policies of reform. It was a waste of time, the *Manchester Guardian* argued, in June 1830, for people to be arguing how the Saxon Witan had been elected; what they should be discussing was what system was most representative of present social needs and best adapted to the present condition of society; a new situation demanded new remedies.[13] Three years later it put forward the principle or slogan that 'reform of all kinds must have a beginning'; the long job of changing the habits of the labouring classes must be tackled, even if this meant, for a start, the provision of those walks and parks so dear to the editor of that newspaper.[14] At the government level, the Mining Commissioners, in 1843, talked of the need to adapt the institutions of the country to ever-changing circumstances and wants, and their best known member, Tremenheere, suggested the following year that a first step had been taken towards a solution of society's problems by a recognition of their existence, though his own identification of 'social disorganisation and moral degradation' did not accord with everyone's view of what they were, even though it agreed with most people's.[15] Mr Slaney had suggested a more humane approach that Parliament might take towards the 'convenience' of the working classes in February 1840, when he had asked for laws to protect their health and comfort, and to safeguard them against commercial fluctuations, as well as making the conventional demands for their education and religious instruction.[16] In even more sympathetic and direct a statement, Lord Ashley, in 1845, enjoined Parliament to fulfil her role as 'a faithful and pious parent'. This required not only that all children should cease to work and have the opportunity to be educated, but that all the advantages of economic progress should be utilised for the 'moral and physical prosperity of the great mass of our people'.[17] These were just a few indications of the growing awareness that reforming policies were now called for, and of some of the areas where they might be applied.

Changed attitudes and policies of reform did not necessarily mean parliamentary legislation and government action. Where the working classes were concerned there was, it was believed, much to be achieved by more humane conduct amongst employers towards their workers. Even with a problem on this enormous scale Dickens seems to have rejected the approach of the fact-finding social investigators, as well as that of the trade union militants, and pinned his faith in human nature to do what was necessary.[18] Job Legh, in *Mary Barton*, was of the opinion that it was not want of power, but want of inclination that caused the bosses to treat their men badly, and on the employers' side, Mr Carson resolved to adopt policies of mutual understanding to improve relations with his men.[19] Similarly, Mr Thornton, in *North and South*, undertook to work for better human relations in industry and declared that 'no mere institutions, however wise . . . can attach class to class . . . unless the working out of such institutions bring the individuals of the different classes into actual personal contact.'[20] This personal contact and industrial paternalism was practised within the colliery community at Flockton, near Wakefield, where a benevolent employer attempted to endear himself to the hearts of his miners by providing them with houses that had gardens attached, promoting a Horticultural (and a Temperance) Society within their midst, providing reading-room facilities in the local school, and organising games for their enjoyment.[21] The same spirit even extended to the profit-sharing schemes so enthusiastically welcomed by William Lovett as an indication that capital and labour were coming together in industrial organisation.[22]

This was an idea or ideal that continued to haunt the imagination and suggest a possible way out of the dilemma of the labour–capital dispute. Employers would make friendly gestures towards their workers and in some way or other successfully establish so harmonious a working relationship with them that problems would all be solved locally and informally, and the state would never need to interfere. It was a notion that relied heavily for its fulfilment on a highly optimistic view of human nature and the willingness and altruism of individuals to act generously without the coercion of the law. Such a view was not justified.

The alternative to it was parliamentary intervention. In the words of one of Charlotte Brontë's troubled workmen, 'Them that governs mun find a way to help us; they mun mak' fresh orderations.'[23] The principles of political economy, however well they were working to promote economic growth, were not at the same time taking care of the social problems that industrialisation was producing, and it was becoming increasingly clear in the 1830s and 1840s that these problems would not solve themselves by a policy of letting well alone and allowing each man to pursue his own individual advantage and thereby ensure the communal good. The idea that all government was a necessary evil would long remain popular, but its necessity would be emphasised by growing numbers, and some, among them Thomas Carlyle, would even come to believe that more, not less, government was the only answer to society's problems.[24] In 1846 Labouchere, in debating the Ten Hour Bill, asked whether it was now to be assumed that all evils were to be tackled, as soon as they had been identified, by legislation.[25] It was a rhetorical question, for the speaker did not accept the need for intervention on this issue, but a fair answer would have been that no such assumption was being made, though governments would increasingly legislate on those questions which seemed amenable to legislation. And as far back as 1830 the *Leeds Mercury*, although a champion of the principles of political economy, had condemned Oastler's original 'factory slaves' letter, written 'with undue warmth and violence', because it was unjust to blame individuals when the fault lay with the law, which allowed children to be overworked. Oastler, said the editor, had better petition for the law to be changed than charge a 'respectable class of manufacturers with hypocrisy and oppression'.[26] This was almost to concede the case for regulation at the outset.

In another quite different sphere, the statistical societies of the early 1830s were stressing upon government, and the upper classes in general, the urgent necessity for reform of the bad conditions of the towns and the bad habits of the people who occupied them, so that there should be no repetition of the cholera scourge of 1832. And if the Poor Law Commissioners of 1834 were engaged in trying to implement some important principles of political economy on the issues of wages and the mobility of labour, they were at the same time creating one of the best known pieces of nineteenth century legislation. The paradox had in fact been foreshadowed in the evidence of a witness who maintained that whilst poverty was 'the allotment of Providence', pauperism was 'the contrivance of man and dependent for its very existence on his impolitic institutions'.[27] It was up to wiser men to contrive more politic institutions, and that meant reform by legislation.

The change towards reforming policies is to be explained in large measure in terms of fear of the working classes, fear of their threat to the nation's health by their insanitary state, and fear of their threat to the nation's political stability by their unsatisfied wants of various kinds. It was a defensive action carried out under threat. A note of panic was to be heard in Leeds, in October 1831, as the local Board of Health issued its instructions on how to cope with the approaching wave of cholera. 'There is a great deal to be done in the eastern parts of the town, in the way of cleansing and ventilating', and in 'some areas in Kirkgate, nests of vice and filth . . . seem certain to prove hot-beds of infection.'[28] The areas in need of attention appear to have been identified quickly enough, but it looks as though the cholera scare had been needed to get action underway. Cholera took its toll and prompted the inevitable 'indignant meeting to demand drainage, proper sewage disposal, and street paving'.[29] John Fielden's cynical view of these proceedings was that the middle classes had flown to working-class houses not from motives of charity, but to save themselves; they had reconstituted a Manchester Board of Health to save their own skins, and, as in the 1795–6 fever scare, the inspiration was not the love of working-class neighbours, but fear of the visitation of God.[30] S. H. Kydd argued similarly, and more tendentiously, in 1857, that factory legislation too had originated in self-preservation as 'disease and death spread among the population'.[31]

Dr Lyon Playfair spoke for the Chadwick approach when he

demanded in 1845 'the interference of a paternal legislation to remedy the evils widely spread and deeply rooted', and added that 'sound economy cannot be in any way opposed to true humanity. . . . I would say that all principles which conduce to the good order and prosperity of the state are involved in the improvement of the sanitary conditions of the population.'[32] In stressing 'economy' as well as 'humanity', he illustrated the nicely balanced arguments characteristic of his time. In 1840, the Health of Towns Commissioners had noted that 'in proportion as the working classes are injuriously affected, so will their value to the community be diminished', whilst the Mining Commissioners were to report in 1845 that it was better 'as a mere matter of calculation . . . to maintain the decencies and proprieties of domestic life'.[33] Economic advantage could make the most necessary reform look even more necessary.

The political threat seemed just as frightening as the threat to health, if a little less tangible and one stage removed. Southey's prediction that the state of the poor, being a great evil, would precipitate civil war if not remedied, was widely echoed.[34] Sir William Molesworth, speaking to the House of Commons, in March 1837, on the inevitable progress of democracy and popular opinion, stressed the need to make that progress harmless and free from political convulsions, and this demanded that the people should be 'at ease and contented'.[35] The safety of the rich was just as important as the welfare of the poor, and the wise mining commissioner, Thomas Tancred, of Northumberland, observed in 1842 that the ancient institutions of the country had not kept pace with the unprecedented changes of recent years. 'We are in a condition of society', he wrote, 'which those institutions were never calculated to meet, and it behoves statesmen, and all who are anxious for our common safety, most seriously and dispassionately to consider how our establishments may be fitted to supply the cravings of that large class of Her Majesty's subjects.'[36] Common safety demanded this.

But if these explanations of the need to implement reform

policies seem to carry a common thread of cynicism, they should be set against the great speech delivered by Macaulay on 22 May 1846, in which he attempted to place the current issue of the Ten Hours Act, and other problems of contemporary politics, within the context of the eternal problem of all governments concerned with the preservation of liberty—the right degree of interference which it was proper for them to exercise. On a purely commercial matter, he said, Parliament would not wish to intervene, but when higher interests were at stake, where morality and humanity were concerned, it would be wrong to adhere to the principle of non-interference. 'It concerns the public weal', he argued, 'that the great mass of the people should not live in a way the effect of which is to abridge life, to make it wretched and feeble while it lasts, and to send to untimely graves the population, who leave behind them a more miserable progeny than themselves.' As lawgivers they must decide what to regulate and what to leave alone, and they had erred, he believed, in the exercise of both parts of their duty. 'We have prevented the labourer from getting his loaf where he could get it cheapest, but we have not prevented him from prematurely destroying the health of his body and mind by inordinate toil.' They had just corrected their wrongful interference; now let them correct their wrongful neglect.[37] Macaulay was not, of course, fixing for all time the position where the line or lines should be drawn; he was simply a highly intelligent Liberal wrestling with the great problem of his age, attempting to suggest appropriate standards for public action under which the dogmatic orthodoxies of the day would be required to yield to both experience and humanity.

For whatever reason, then, a need was increasingly being felt to 'do something for the workers', though there were some who persisted in the view that all that was needed was for the Corn Laws to be repealed and all would then be fine, and it was a characteristic of all parliamentary debates in the 1830s and 1840s which attempted to deal with the social conditions of the poor, that some free trader would join the debate and offer free

trade in corn as the grand panacea for the workers' troub
Even Sir William Molesworth's speech of 1837, on the need fc
contented working class, had moved on to the proposition th
'everything should be removed which tends hurtfully to limit
the field of employment', and that kind of reference was
intended for one subject in particular.[38] Dr Kay had maintained
in 1832 that the manufacturers 'ranked among the foremost
advocates of every measure to remove the pressure of public
burden from the people', and the Factory Commissioners
themselves had considered as an alternative to shortening hours
the suggestion of making it easier for the working classes to
earn their living by removing taxes.[39] But these ideas, the
extension of the principles of political economy, were usually
part of the propaganda of the free traders rather than a serious
attempt to tackle the working-class problem as such, and many
free traders, including Kay himself, were aware of the need to
do much more than abolish the bread tax.

The decision on what to do was determined primarily by
response to the basic question cited earlier of whether the
problems of the poor were thought to be mainly the result of
industrialisation or of urbanisation. Not surprisingly, most of
the industrialists blamed the towns, but there were some,
Robert Peel the Elder, Robert Owen, and John Fielden, for
example, who were prepared to accept their own share of the
responsibility and who urged their fellow employers to accept
regulations. Peel had persuaded Parliament to accept responsibility for the treatment of pauper apprentices by his Health
and Morals of Apprentices Act of 1802, and he successfully
campaigned for the political extension of this principle to 'free
labour' after the war. In the debate of 1816, Mr Wrottesley
accepted that 'if there were 99 manufacturers well regulated,
while the 100th was in a different state, that alone would
authorise the exertions of Parliament', and Peel's Act of 1819
did at least make it illegal for children under nine to work in
cotton mills, and restricted children at work to a twelve hour
day.[40] There were minor alterations made to the law in the

1820s, but in 1830 Richard Oastler's great popular campaign for a Ten Hour Bill began. The Bill was not passed until 1847, but produced in the short run the celebrated Factory Act of 1833, by which no child under nine could work in any textile mill, save silk and lace, and under which restrictions were placed upon the working hours of all children and young persons. A provision was inserted for two hours' schooling for children, and inspectors were appointed to see that the Act was carried out.

This Act, with all its limitations in the eyes of its critics, was a major breach in the policy of non-interference, and allocated the state a responsibility and a role which would later be extended to cover the working conditions of adults as well as children. John Fielden, who bitterly resented the attacks of Dr Kay and others on working-class morality as slanders and libels on the working man, argued that it was not their hearts that needed restraint but their bodies which required respite; the factory system of overworking, which led to disease, depression, drinking and drug-taking, was the basic cause of the working-class condition, and Factory Acts were the means to tackle the problem; the manufacturers must be made to consent to regulation, as Coleridge had argued some years earlier.[41] But Fielden, and Oastler too, would have gone much further than Factory Acts in providing for the welfare of the industrial workforce, and wished Parliament to assume a more complete responsibility for the economy, not only protecting the factory workers but safeguarding the interests of domestic workers threatened with redundancy, intervening to keep up their wages, and taking a national responsibility on such matters as technological change to ensure that mechanisation was not allowed where it was detrimental to the interests of large numbers of people. The Oastler ideal of an almost omnicompetent state with full responsibility for supervising the course of economic change, in which competition and profit were replaced by considerations of morality or 'public interest', had, of course, no chance of realisation. Factory reform was the one practical achievement of men of this outlook, but this has been widely adjudged as one of the great stabilising features within nineteenth-century society, and one of the chief means by which the working classes were reconciled to industrialisation.

Many contemporaries believed that factory reform was largely irrelevant to the needs of the working classes and directed their energies to the conditions of the towns as the alternative explanation of working-class depression. The viewpoint was clearly put by Joseph Hume, in April 1845, when he urged MPs to remember that whilst they had been engaged in their party squabbles, enquiries set up by themselves had established that people in the towns were living in filth, squalor, and misery that was almost incredible, had it not been so distinctly proved. It would, he said, be a more practical course for them to follow if they were to tackle these problems instead of trying to control the hours of labour.[42] Urban reform was offered as an alternative to factory reform. Its origin was the cholera scare of 1831 and epidemic of 1832, which prompted the establishment of local Boards of Health in the industrial towns, through which local doctors, such as Baker of Leeds, famed for his maps of cholera incidence, took stock of the local situation. The statistical societies that came into being at the same time—one in Manchester was the first in 1833—also pursued their quest for detailed knowledge and added to the demand for sanitary reform. Without a satisfactory urban environment, society would be repeatedly threatened by epidemic disease, and industry would be denied the services of a healthy and contented workforce. And so Dr Kay, a leading advocate of urban reform, was able to list the manufacturers amongst the 'most active promoters of every plan conducive to physical improvement or moral elevation'.[43] It was in their own interest that their workforce should be well-housed and physically robust, and so their attention was directed towards the environmental factors encountered in the towns.

According to G. R. Porter, the first secretary of the statistical department of the Board of Trade, there had been, by 1846, a

K   147

decade of great and growing interest in the condition of society, and efforts made to better the physical condition of the labouring classes.[44] The question was, in Edwin Chadwick's view, 'how far the physical evils by which the health, and strength, and morals of the labouring classes are depressed may be removed . . . by private and voluntary exertions'; there was clearly a limit to individual enterprise, and Chadwick put forward in his great report 'the facts which serve to show how far the aid of the legislature and of administrative arrangements are requisite' for making the habitations of the poor and the streets of their towns more sanitary places.[45] Such sanitary evils as existed, according to the *Manchester Guardian* in March 1846, arose from inattention or ignorance, not from any want of will to remove them once they had been identified, and Joseph Hume was to declare portentiously in March 1847, that no self-interested association should be allowed to stand in the way of any general improvements demanded by the public.[46]

The sentiments were noble enough, but the practice fell some way below them. In February 1843, Sir James Graham assured Parliament that the government agreed on the desirability of preventing interment in cities, and the need to improve drains and the mode of building, yet eighteen months later, Mr Mackinnon asked why the House should go to the expense of committees and commissions if the government was not going to act over the acknowledged evil of interment in towns.[47] Governmental feet were certainly dragged over this question of sanitary reform, which reached the stage of legislation only in 1848 with Morpeth's Public Health Act, a typically Victorian compromise which recognised an evil, and permitted, but did not compel, action to be taken over it. Local Health Boards were allowed to pursue sanitary reforms, and a General Board in London was to advise but not to direct them. The ineffective nature of this legislation, and the very slow progress made generally in the field of public health by mid-century, even in the dismal lack of provision for public walks, parks, and gardens which had exercised the minds of the well-intentioned for so long, together suggest that this environmental reform should not be rated too highly as a factor in reconciling the working classes to industrialisation. Public health was in its merest infancy, and civic pride even in the second half of the nineteenth century was to be expressed in terms of town halls rather than better housing for the working classes.

Perhaps it is important to recognise intent as well as achievement, or its absence. Lord John Manners, speaking on the Ten Hour Bill, in May 1846, as a benevolent, paternalistic Tory, made an interesting appraisal of the issue of reform in relation to the needs of the working classes.

> I look forward with joyful anticipation to the time when the working men of this wealth-ridden country shall be able to regard with just feelings of pride and gratitude a House of Commons that thought its highest duty and its dearest wish was to minister to the wants, direct the wishes, listen to the prayers, increase the comforts, diminish the toil, and elevate the character of the long-suffering, industrious, and gallant people of England.[48]

His heart was in the right place, but his political theory would soon be out-of-date.

But of all the reforms offered to the working classes in the nineteenth century, that which supposedly contained the most healing properties was education, and it is most surprising, in view of the wonders that education was expected to work, that its extension was left in the hands of the Sunday schools, the religious organisations, and the ancient foundations, and that no new schools were built by public bodies until the creation of school boards under the Forster Act of 1870. The *Manchester Guardian* praised the government for its first grant of £20,000 of public funds to the two religious organisations, the National Society and the British and Foreign Society, which were undertaking school-building; the more cynical contrasted this with the £20,000,000 paid out in the same year as compensation to the West Indian slave owners.[49] In 1841, when the annual grant had increased by 50% to £30,000, an MP reported frequent complaints which he had heard about the size of this sum in comparison with the £70,000 which the government had spent on the royal stables at Windsor in 1839, and a further disgruntled MP, Mr Smith O'Brien, complained that there was probably no instance on record of a country with so much wealth doing so little to promote intellectual matters.[50] Still, it was possible for G. R. Porter to record in 1846 in his *Progress of the Nation* that, 'we may now feel assured that the cause of enlightenment is, humanly speaking, placed beyond the reach of injury from the conflicts of party', though he was less sanguine, and justifiably so, about the ability of a public education to emerge free from all sectarian objectives, an unhappily prophetic piece of gloom.[51]

Education was something like sanitary reform, a good thing for a variety of odd reasons. An apparently naïve William Howitt rejoiced in the growth of schools, mechanics institutes, libraries, and other plans on the part of the wealthy for the benefit of the poor, because they would make available to the poor pleasures of a higher order, a delight in books, in their homes and families, and in the glorious face of Nature. 'We are creatures of new circumstance', he enthused, 'and of a higher reach of knowledge.'[52] This might have accorded with the ideas of H. G. Wells half a century later; it would not do for his contemporaries, who had far more mundane purposes to pursue in dispensing this commodity of education amongst the working classes. Like the healthy worker, the educated worker was a more valuable property to his employer than the uneducated one, as commissioner R. D. Grainger reported in 1842.[53] If only the working classes would cultivate the intellect and not the senses by making better use of their leisure, urged the *Manchester Guardian* in 1824, they would become richer, and there could be no greater incentive than wealth, especially in Manchester.[54]

But an educated worker was not only a richer and more

efficient worker; he was also, contrary to what had once been supposed, a safer member of society and one less likely to disturb the social system in which he had his being. Culture was offered by Thomas Arnold as the alternative to anarchy; education was required by people before poverty played havoc with them.[55] Dr Kay had put the point more crudely when he urged 'the rearing of hardy and intelligent working men, whose character and habits shall afford the largest amount of security to the property and order of the community.'[56] It was a mistake, argued Mr Roebuck MP, in 1833, to think of education as dangerous to the peace of the country and the security of property: it would serve quite the opposite purpose.[57] And an Assistant Commissioner on Handloom Weaving was to report in 1840–1 that only by instruction could the unskilled be redeemed from vice and misery, and that education should be fostered as much out of concern for the peace of society as for the moral improvement of those who would receive it.[58]

It might reasonably be asked what kind of education people had in mind which was to achieve such ends by its establishment. It was desirable, according to a report by the Commission on Child Employment from Gloucester in 1842, that 'the rising generation of operatives should acquire a more general tone of correct feeling, sound intelligence and practical piety' than were currently being achieved, the 'correct feeling' being perhaps the same thing that the *Manchester Guardian* had had in mind in 1833 when arguing for a national system of education to 'lay the axe to a thousand prejudices'.[59] Not all the 'thousand prejudices' were itemised by the supporters of education, but some of them were. Dr Kay thought that the 'ascertained truths of political science should be early taught to the labouring classes, and correct political information should be constantly and industriously disseminated amongst them', a most daunting prospect for the workers.[60] Dr Ure had very similar notions that the 'misconceptions which operatives entertain as to the real effect of machinery on the price of labour' could be educated away and that artisans could be taught to live temperately, husband their earnings, and place their surplus funds to advantage.[61] In other words, workers could be taught to become models of their employers and share all their values. Roebuck, too, though looking to the more distant future and the 'slow operation of time, patience, and industry', believed that education would be valuable for teaching people what they could expect a government to do and what they must expect to have to do for themselves. 'Let them once understand thoroughly their social condition, and we shall have no more unmeaning discontents, no wild and futile schemes of Reform . . . we shall have right efforts directed to right ends.'[62]

It all sounds rather grim, though doubtless this was not intended by middle-class men, who believed that the best service they could perform for the workers and for themselves was to inculcate into the working men those excellent values of which they themselves were so proud. If the workers would only become more sober, more moral, more diligent, more thrifty, more appreciative of the value of savings banks, they would then start to use their leisure sensibly, and, hopefully, take a modest and realistic view of their political position; for so much of their energy would be devoted to pursuing virtuous lives that they would have no time for the vain phantom attractions of politics. This was Dr Kay's view in 1832, and it was represented more sympathetically twenty years later by Tremenheere, the Mining Commissioner, in the light of abortive political endeavour from the working classes in Chartism and a distinct recognition on his part that the more brutalising aspects of life were being tackled. His experiences in the 1840s had taken him into some of the grimmest and most primitive societies throughout Britain, where he had found almost sub-human conditions prevailing. Now he felt that the corner had been turned. There was still a threat to social stability in that the workers were beginning to find their feet through trade unionism and Chartism, but the threat was no longer that of anarchical violence which could have erupted earlier. The workers had settled down to some extent, but the battle was very much on for men's minds, their loyalties, and their affections. The great issues for him now were religion and education, by which the defeats of trade unionism and Chartism might be consolidated into a settled and steady sharing by the working classes of the attitudes and values of their social superiors.[63] It was the same hope as Kay's, but a more realistic one after the passing of the troubled decades of the 1830s and 1840s.

Arguably, of course, it was all a great confidence trick. Cobbett had, in 1830, attacked the Society for the Diffusion of Useful Knowledge on the grounds that like all the rest of the educational schemes it was a combination for the purpose of amusing the working classes and diverting their attention from the true causes of their poverty and misery.[64] Engels had a similar thing to say later about the mechanics institutes, that they were providing education in those fields of study that were thought likely to wean the workers away from opposition to the middle classes.[65] The workers were encouraged to imbibe the middle-class ethic, and to want those things which the middle classes wanted. Sociologists recognise this as a process of embourgeoisement among the working classes, and it is difficult to resist the conclusion that such policies were not without considerable success.

That great vice of the early financiers, their commercialism and their materialistic outlook, was not to remain for ever the prerogative of one social class. Wealth is most sordid to those who do not possess it, and if it becomes more widely dispersed, its vicious propensities seem to decline. The Select Committee on Handloom Weavers' Petitions were told in 1834 by R. M. Martin, that the mass of the people would disregard abstract principles if they were well fed.[66] Nothing but questions of domestic comfort and employment would rouse the workers to violence, reported the Mining Commissioner, Thomas Tancred, in 1843, and the history of Chartism, the 'bread and butter' question, went some way towards justifying this interpretation.[67] Thomas Cooper, the former Chartist leader from

Leicester, visited Lancashire later in the century and found the Lancastrians talking of nothing but their shares in co-operative or building societies.[68] William Morris would implore working men not to be satisfied by modest prosperity but to seek a just society and open their eyes to what the real joys of life could be.[69] But the visionaries with their eternal verities never delivered their just societies except in print, and working men settled for a kind of living—creatures as philistine as the bosses who had made them. In December 1835, the *Manchester Guardian* urged the 'extreme desirableness of making the labouring classes the ministers to their own respectability and improvement', and suggested savings banks and annuity societies as the means towards accomplishing this.[70] Thirty years later the president of the Reform League was declaring that,

> the working classes themselves are deeply interested in the preservation of law and order, of the rights of capital and property; of the honour and power of our country. They are as members of co-operative, building, and other societies, daily becoming capitalists and land-owners; there are among them men of large intellectual capacity and earnest unaffected christian principle.[71]

What historians have on the whole been able to recognise is a process by which, as industrialisation made its benefits more generally available, the original organs of working-class protest became 'institutionalised', were found a place within the system, and acquired the ambiguous function of looking after working-class interests, a system which the working class were consolidating by their willingness to participate in its operation.[72] The protesting organisations continued to protest, up to a point, but they began to have so much in common with the object of their protest that they would never try seriously to dislodge it. And so capitalism found its surest bulwarks in the chapels, the friendly societies, the co-operative societies, the trade unions, and, eventually and conclusively, in the Labour Party.

It is much too early to attempt any conclusive assessment of the role of Methodism in working-class history. On the one hand historians have stressed the political and industrial techniques which the working classes learnt from their membership of the Methodist movement and how leaders emerged on the labour side who had received their early training within Methodist classes. On the other hand contemporaries were ready to see the advantages that society might derive from having a well-disciplined, Methodist-trained working class which would remain quiescent during times of political upheaval and would adapt itself obediently to the requirements of the new industrial system. Cobbett's condemnation of the Methodists as the 'bitterest foes of freedom', and Dr Ure's eloquent defence of Methodism as the ideal religion for a successful industrial concern, both supported the view that the influence of Methodism was very much on the conservative side, and if many former Methodists eventually found their way into trade union organisation and labour politics, it is clear that the organisations they helped to create were designed to change society by reformist means, not overthrow it by revolutionary ones.[73] And so, even a couple of generations beyond the French Revolution, the Methodist movement was still exercising a moderating influence on the working class movement, no longer turning potential radicals away from politics to religion, as could be argued in relation to its earlier role, but sending men of religion into politics to practise zealously the non-violent ways which they had acquired from their religious teaching.[74] In this way the chapels made at least a two-fold contribution to reconciling the working classes to nineteenth century industrial society, providing the workers for a long time with institutions where they could feel at home, and later providing them with teachers who would help to ensure for them a reasonable share of the profits that were made.

The friendly societies also served a similar purpose, giving working men a peaceful outlet for their social activities and encouraging them in thrift and independence, two highly prized virtues in the competitive, capitalist society to which they were adjusting. Although the early societies certainly provided some cover for illicit trade union activity after the Combination Laws of 1799–1800, they primarily offered members an insurance against the possibility of sickness, and cover for their eventual burial expenses. The government approved of them in that they removed some of the strain from rising poor rates, and fostered self-help amongst the working classes, which was to be encouraged in that it extended the range of social groups accepting and practising the new system of values. By 1815 the friendly societies were believed to involve almost a million people, and their membership ran well ahead of the trade unions' throughout the nineteenth century. They were able to tighten up their organisation and efficiency, and in 1849 a select committee which investigated them reported that, 'Of late years by the exertions of benevolent persons and by means of a more extensive and accurate collection of statistical materials, better information has been obtained and diffused of the calculations and principles upon which such societies ought to be based.'[75] The friendly society was almost the characteristic working-class response to industrialisation; it ameliorated its harshest consequences yet it owed its very existence to it.

And the same could equally be said of the co-operative societies, which made economic survival for the working man an easier business and at the same time gave him a vested interest in the success and prosperity of an important social institution. The ironies attached to the evolution of the co-operative idea have been frequently pointed out; a movement, begun by Robert Owen to change society by building model communities of moral regeneration, ended up at the very heart of the society it was to leave behind, and serving a quite different purpose. The profit-sharing retailing which was originally for the purpose of raising money to buy land, a means to an end, became the end itself, and co-operation became a matter of shop-keeping and not community building.[76] The existing community was accepted, and the workers were identified with yet another institution within it, which was their own and advantageous to them.

The history of trade unionism in the nineteenth century, though vastly more complicated, is not without strong similarities; the Amalgamated Society of Engineers, the model of the 'New Model' unions, is said to have done for trade unionism what the Rochdale Pioneers did for the co-operative movement.[77] In the 1830s, trade unionism, especially in its general union phase, was, like co-operation, concerned to change the world, or at least to overthrow capitalism and change the nature of British society. By the middle of the century the picture had altered dramatically. Trade unionism had reverted to traditional practice and was once more exclusively the preserve of skilled workers who practised good capitalist economics of selling their product as dearly as possible, becoming aware of the scarcity value of what they had to offer. The trade unions belonged to those groups of workers, builders, engineers, miners, iron and steel workers, or skilled textile workers, a labour 'aristocracy' who had done very well out of the Industrial Revolution, and who had a vested interest in perpetuating the new society, and exploiting it to their own advantage.[78] The morality of capitalism, the despair of people like Coleridge or Oastler in former times, had become the morality of the skilled workers, and the unskilled were left to fend for themselves. The unions largely abstained from radical political involvement and even invested their funds in the capitalist concerns that gave them employment. They became acceptable and respectable, acquired the confidence of employers, and if they became the means by which the employers were controlled by the workers, they became just as surely the means by which the workers were controlled by the employers, in a relationship of apparently mutual advantage based on the acceptance of those developments which had made it all

157

possible, the capitalist Industrial Revolution. Grievances inevitably remained, but they were tackled through the machinery that trade unionism now provided, rather than by machine-breaking or some other form of industrial sabotage from earlier days. Again, here were specifically working-class institutions which owed their form and their power to industrialisation, and were the means by which economic change was exploited to working-class advantage.

In this way almost all the specifically working-class organisations and institutions, which developed in the nineteenth century as part of the working-class response to industrialisation, ended up as characteristic institutions of the industrial state, seeking to soften it, to civilise it, to exploit it, but not to overthrow it. The working classes, who suffered most, though not, of course, uniformly, from the process of industrialisation, eventually emerged as the guardians of the industrial state, for as they attained the appropriate degree of affluence and respectability they were rewarded with the vote. And if, as some claim, there still remains a psychological reluctance to accept the idea that Britain has ever industrialised, a reluctance nourished on 'a diet of the Bible, Shakespeare, and the Pastoral poets', the emotional and sentimental objections to the industrial world, and expressed preferences for some other kind of existence, do not come from the working classes.[79]

Notes to this chapter are on page 185.

7 The Industrial Revolution and the Historians

For all the importance of the words and deeds of men and women of the past, it can be argued, not without reason, that history is made by historians as much as by anyone. It is certainly true that what people know of the past they learn mostly from what historians have written about it, and so it would be unrealistic to consider contemporary views and judgments on the process of Industrial Revolution without some recognition of how historians have felt about it. And historians, in being human and in properly fulfilling their function, have become involved in the arguments about industrialisation not simply as recorders but as participants in the debate on the merits and demerits of industrialised society.

It would be very convenient if these arguments could be neatly categorised, if, for instance, it were possible to distinguish those that were purely academic from those that were largely ideological, those that were of recent origin from those that were current at the time of industrialisation, those that were continuing from those that had now been resolved. Unfortunately, this kind of categorisation is barely possible, since it seems to be true of almost all the major controversies that they are of long-standing, unresolved, and an almost inseparable mixture of academic with ideological considerations. The social scientists who are today still attempting to solve the mystery of the population explosion, or who are investigating nineteenth-century towns with such scholarly thoroughness and detail, are bringing to their work techniques of study and a precision traditionally associated with scientific investigation.[1] Factual controversies concerning, for instance, the extent to which the landed interests invested in the new industry seem, to the non-specialist at least, not to be overflowing with ideological content however much passion they are capable of arousing in those with a specialist interest.[2] But the same cannot be said of most other controversial issues.

And where ideological commitment has not taken over, there is often an emotional involvement that determines the nature of judgments passed, the psychological reluctance already noted to accept the fact of industrialisation, the belief that the Industrial Revolution was the second fall of man and that his state of sin has doubled in intensity since that change in his existence. The search for 'the world we have lost', a scholarly and entertaining undertaking when pursued in the spirit of disciplined enquiry, can so easily become merely a sentimental journey.[3] It is difficult to be neutral where the Industrial Revolution is concerned.

The enclosure controversy epitomises the rural side of the debate on industrialisation, as supporters and opponents of enclosure and industrialisation have disagreed over the motives, methods, and results associated with the changes in landholding and usage. The opponents have seen enclosure as a crude device for creating a mobile labour force, and the Hammonds, for instance, talked of dispossessed small farmers driven into the towns to fill the new factories.[4] The supporters on the other hand have supplied benevolent for wicked motivation in arguing that the main pressure towards enclosure was the need to provide more food for a growing population.[5] The former stressed the rapacious nature of larger landowners, the inhumanity of enclosing commissioners, and the injustices of their procedures as the great 'land swindle' was perpetrated.[6] The latter, believing that more rational and productive methods of agriculture were a sufficiently important end to justify means that were occasionally questionable, have at the same time found the owners and commissioners much more equitable and much less arbitrary than was often supposed. The law was enforced and legal rights upheld. The results of this enforcement have led some to continue to look for the social distress and upheavals arising from it. The supporters of enclosure have minimised the former and denied the existence of the latter, and enclosure has been allocated a very subordinate role amongst the causes of rural rioting during the first half of the nineteenth century. The principle problem of the country-side was not enclosure, but the fact that population was growing in excess of the demand for rural labour, in spite of the increased numbers needed to produce more food, and these surplus people either remained behind as a rural problem or migrated to the towns. An urban labour force was thus derived from the natural increase of the countryside, not the result of dispossession, and the new towns provided an opportunity for survival which the countryside no longer did. The element of coercion remains in the argument, but an impersonal force has replaced the personal one.

The still controversial factory debate is the urban counter-part of the argument on enclosure, and factories retain their symbolic importance in the history of industrialisation. Some historians feel that the early factories were in their day a scape-goat for all the ills and evils of an industrialising country.[7] They are still in many ways the touchstone issue, so much so, that one distinguished historian T. S. Ashton, has been attacked by another, Christopher Hill, for the degree of detachment he was able to maintain on aspects of a question over which commitment is apparently almost a requirement.[8] Motiva-tion, methods, and results are all again at issue. Some argue that the workers had almost to be driven into factories, and emphasise the unpopularity of the institutions and the nature of the early labour force, the pauper apprentices and the social outcasts; others stress that this was a quickly passing phase and emphasise the attractions of high wages which brought the workers flocking to the towns. Some stress the cruelties and inhumanity of the early factories, especially child-employment, whilst others emphasise how quickly improvements took place and how impossible it has always been to ascertain the actual consequences of factory employment for the health and physique of those who performed there. What to some people has appeared to be cruel and oppressive conduct on behalf of the early factory masters has to others appeared the necessary disciplining of wage labour, a difficult problem with which the inexperienced owners had to deal. Sympathies tend to be shown either to the workers or their employers; a defence of one often involves a villification of the other and the balanced approach is not always easy to find or even welcomed when it is attempted.[9]

Again, as with enclosure, the human factor has now been played down. Individuals, with personal motivation, have lost much of the responsibility for the factory problem, and modern inclination is to look to the pressure of uncontrollable circumstances, such as speed of change or inexperience, for an explanation of problems and to the passage of time for their solution. Even the Factory Acts, traditionally held to be great measures of amelioration and reconciliation, have been attacked as a counter-productive interference by do-gooders who should have been prepared to let the problems solve themselves in their own good time.[10]

There has in fact been a changed approach of late on the whole question of the social and administrative reforms which industrialisation made necessary and which governments began to implement from the 1830s. This has arisen from the so-called 'growth of government controversy', which itself arose from the apparently neutral and innocuous investigations of the processes by which reform was achieved in particular administrative branches. From Oliver MacDonagh's enquiries into conditions of passenger transport ships, a whole school of thought has arisen which questions the traditional view that credit for reform should go to reformers in general and Benthamites in particular.[11] The rival view is that society as a whole was capable of recognising an intolerable situation and generating an administrative impulse towards rectifying it. This view has been described as a 'Tory interpretation' of history, though it is almost a philosophy of the nature of change, and has enormous implications for the whole study of the Industrial Revolution.[12] Its critics maintain the traditional view that social evils are caused by the actions of bad men and cured by the actions of good ones; the Industrial Revolution was socially so disastrous because wicked and greedy men perpetrated so many evils upon their fellow-creatures. If there is no credit or blame to apportion, the industrialists must be excused their various sins of commission and omission for which they have been traditionally blamed, industrial change must be seen to generate solutions in the same way as it generated problems, and the whole process of industrialisation stands in danger of losing much of its capacity for provoking disagreement. Naturally such a view of the past is not going unchallenged, and consensus history seems no more realistic a concept than consensus politics.

This is particularly true of the controversies concerning the implication of industrialisation for the development of social class in Great Britain, in which historians are being assisted by the insights of sociologists, if occasionally bemused by their technical vocabulary. The working classes, the largest social entity to owe its modern existence to industrialisation, have attracted most attention, which has of late focused specifically on the extent to which a politically self-conscious working class emerged from the working classes during the closing years of the eighteenth and early decades of the nineteenth century. Traditional views of class, as an indication of role within the social and economic systems, have been extended by Edward Thompson to embrace the sense of a common experience, and his study of *The Making of the English Working Class* has done more to disturb the calm of British historiography than any work since Namier's.[13] Whilst one man shocked by taking ideology out of politics, the other shocked by the passion with which he restored it. In keeping with the main traditions surrounding controversies associated with industrialisation, this latest has provoked charges and counter-charges of partisan behaviour and ideological commitment, and these seem likely to attend the efforts that are being made to refine the concept of class-consciousness and to explain its varying degrees of intensity in different economic settings.[14]

And in the emergence or non-emergence, as the case may be, of an English working class, the role of Methodism has remained supremely controversial, if slightly more academic an issue than the larger question. Contributions to this debate have sometimes seemed to be determined by a liking for or dislike of Methodism, similarly conflicting emotions about religion in general, or about the desirability of revolution, or even about the desirability of the working classes.[15]

But the biggest debate of all and the one that comprehends almost all other disagreements about the desirability or otherwise of the Industrial Revolution is that concerning the standard of living experienced by the working classes who lived through the years of greatest economic and social upheaval. The intricacies and refinements of argument involved in this debate are considerable, but it would probably not be oversimplifying too much to distinguish two main approaches to it, that of the historians who see the economic growth achieved during the Industrial Revolution as a mighty performance which excuses some of the social defects which accompanied it, and that of the social critics whose interest is primarily in the state of society and these very social defects, and who are less interested in the economic achievement. There are, of course, historians who see some virtue in both sides.[16]

The champions of economic growth emphasise that it was only because of the Industrial Revolution that Britain was able to escape from a situation, such as existed in the late seventeenth century, whereby half of the people were permanently paupers because there was not enough work for them to do, and death through famine was a regular occurrence. As a result of industrialisation, starvation and mass poverty have disappeared from this country and remained to plague only those countries which have so far failed to convert to an industrial economy. Not only did industrialisation achieve this; it did so whilst the country was experiencing an unprecedented population explosion, allowed it to survive this ordeal without the accompaniment of social anarchy arising from hunger and economic depression, and brought substantial material advantages to an ever-growing population who have come to expect, demand, and enjoy an ever-rising standard of living.[17]

The social critics for their part can hardly deny these propositions, but suggest that the achievement of economic growth, great though this was, should not be seen as an end in itself and that it was attained at such a high social cost that the whole exercise becomes questionable. Their primary concern is to assess the quality of the new civilisation rather than to measure its economic prosperity, and the important issues for them are concerned with the lives of the people, their new experience of town-dwelling and factory labour, the new status of wage-labourer, and the curtailment of personal freedom that the individual might have experienced. They question the happiness of people and the justice of the new social arrangements. It is right, says E. P. Thompson, that value judgments should be passed on 'the whole process entailed in the Industrial Revolution of which we ourselves are an end product', and a whole tradition has evolved of social historians who have fulfilled the additional role of social critic.[18]

It could be argued that these two groups of people are talking about different things, that each is interpreting the role of the historian in its own way and that there is insufficient common ground between them for a genuine argument to take place or agreement to be reached. Up to a point they do go their separate ways, but they also come together on the more precise issue of whether, in the short run, the Industrial Revolution brought an immediate rise in living standards to those workers who were actually living through it. This issue is an attempt to deal with quantifiable factors, items that can be measured, rather than those, like happiness, which are purely abstract. J. L. and Barbara Hammond, prominent members of the social criticism school, attempted to bolster their case in 1917 by maintaining that the half century following the outbreak of the

French wars witnessed a great increase in national wealth, yet at the same time an increase in working-class poverty; no share of the increased wealth went to the workers and the standard of life for the poor was actually depressed.[19] They were answered by J. H. Clapham in 1926, who used the available statistics on wages and prices to argue a contrary case; in industries apart from the dying trades such as handloom weaving, wage rates rose in the period 1780–1850 on average by 40% and in the same period the cost of living fell slightly, so living standards must have risen.[20] Clapham's statistics were in their turn subjected to criticism, largely for their incompleteness, and historians are still arguing whether enough is known about actual wages as opposed to wage-rates, unemployment and underemployment, the wages of the unskilled as opposed to the skilled workers, food prices, and other items of expenditure such as rents, consumption patterns and regional and possibly seasonal variations in many of these factors to permit the compilation of an agreed index of wages or the cost of living.[21]

And in the absence of agreement on what the statistics can prove, historians have suggested theoretical considerations on which to base their case; the extent to which wages might have been kept down by an over-abundant labour supply; or the profit-motivation of employers and investors which prompted a redistribution of wealth and increased inequality; the extent to which current consumption was sacrificed to the needs of capital investment; the possibility that population was growing faster than production, or that Britain's overseas customers were reaping the advantages, through favourable terms of trade, rather than Britain's workers; and the extent to which the state redressed the balance of wealth by taxation and social provision.[22] And the beauty of the theoretical consideration is that it is just as difficult to disprove as it is to prove, and so the argument remains unresolved. Agreement has been achieved only about the fate of select groups of workers or the trends of short periods of time: the improving standards of the skilled workers; the decline of the weavers and the stockingers after their early share in the general prosperity of the late eighteenth century; and the deteriorating standards which prevailed during the period of the French wars.[23] To these propositions there is a fairly general assent, but a final reckoning seems a remote prospect. And if this is true on the statistical side of the dispute, how much more true it must be on these non-quantifiable aspects of change which are for some the issues of real importance. If a tentative verdict is sought on what were the issues of real importance, it would have to be admitted that the working classes have themselves settled for prosperity rather than justice, and if industrialisation is to be judged for its ability to provide the former rather than the latter, then its beneficial consequences must be acknowledged.

Yet the feeling persists, among historians as well as laymen, that the debate on industrialisation is not, at bottom, a discussion about standards of living but on ways of life. R. M. Hartwell's call for a new methodology that will permit comparisons between different ways of life and so make possible 'a final calculation of welfare', or E. P. Thompson's demand for a moral judgment on the process of industrial change which has led to the creation of present day society, both seem to imply a reaching out towards some standard of assessment, other than a material one, that will set a final seal of approval or disapproval upon the Industrial Revolution, the most significant development in 2,000 years of human history.[24] Until such an agreed criterion is found, industrialisation will continue to seem to some people of the present day, as it seemed to contemporaries, a development by which people were driven from the open countryside into overcrowded and unhealthy towns, and living and working became separated functions of human existence. Nor will it be possible to counter these views with crude accusations of nostalgia and romanticism, for they represent regrets and yearnings very central to the predicament of modern man.

Notes to this chapter are on page 188.

Notes to Chapters

1 The Industrial Revolution and Contemporary Awareness

1 Postgate, R. W. *The Builders' History* (1923), pp 12–13
2 Clark, G. N. 'The Idea of the Industrial Revolution', David Murray Foundation Lecture (Glasgow, 1952)
3 Koebner, R. 'Adam Smith and the Industrial Revolution', *Economic History Review*, 2nd series, vol 11 (1959)
4 *Manchester Mercury* (9 July, 1811); 'Report of Committee on Silk Ribbon Weavers' Petitions' (1818), p 116
5 Engels, F. *Condition of the Working Class in England* (1958 ed), p 57
6 *Manchester Guardian* (19 December, 1834); Kay, J. P. *The Moral and Physical Condition of the Working Classes* (1832), 1969 ed, p 76
7 Galt, J. *Annals of the Parish* (1821), p 189
8 *The Commercial Directory, 1814–15*, p 72
9 'Report of Factory Commissioners, 1833, Western District', p 2
10 'Report of Select Committee on Health of Towns, 1840', p iii
11 *Torrington Diaries 1781–1794* (1934 ed), vol 2, p 179
12 *Nottingham Journal* (29 January, 1785)
13 Parliamentary Debates, vol 41 (9 December 1819), p 953
14 '1st Report of Municipal Corporations Commissioners, 1835', pp 1507, 1758, 1572
15 Ibid, vol 21 (18 January, 1812), p 181
16 Cobbett, W. *Rural Rides* (1830), 1967 ed, p 286
17 *Manchester Guardian* (14 July, 1821; 11 June, 1831)
18 Ibid (18 July, 1834)
19 '1st Report of Select Committee on Combinations of Workmen, 1838', p 165; '17th Report of Select Committee on Poor Law Amendment Act, 1838', p 3
20 'Report of Select Committee on Handloom Weavers' Petitions, 1834', p 267; 'Reports from Assistant Handloom Weavers' Commissioners, 1839', p 19; Habakkuk, H. J. *American and British Technology in the 19th Century* (1962)

21 'Report of Poor Law Commissioners 1834', appendix A, p 914
22 'Report of the Commissioners on the State of the Population in Mining Districts, 1844, Scotland and parts of Staffordshire', pp 15–16
23 'Report of Poor Law Commissioners, 1834', p 199
24 'Report of Committee on State of Woollen Manufacture, 1806', p 440
25 Parl Debs, 3rd series, vol 39 (30 November, 1837), p 381; 'Report of Select Committee on Health of Towns, 1840', p iv
26 Parl Debs, 3rd series, vol 20 (19 March, 1834), p 438
27 Laslett, P. *The World We Have Lost* (1965), 1968 ed, p 212
28 Ogden, J. *Manchester A Hundred Years Ago 1783* (ed Axon, 1887), p 16
29 Galt, J. *Annals of the Parish*, p 177
30 *Nottingham Journal* (18 October, 1794)
31 'Report of Minutes of Evidence before Select Committee on Children's Employment in Manufactories of the United Kingdom, 1816', p 15
32 'Report of Inspectors of Factories, January, 1839, James Stuart'
33 Parl Debs, vol 40 (14 June, 1819), p 1132; 'Report of Minutes of Evidence before Select Committee on Children's Employment in Manufactories of the United Kingdom, 1816', p 141
34 Parl Debs, vol 6 (12 March, 1806), p 424
35 'Report from Commissioners on Framework knitters, 1845, Nottinghamshire', p 29
36 Ashton, T. S. *The Industrial Revolution* (1948), 1968 ed, p 48
37 eg Ibid, pp 72–5
38 *Nottingham Journal* (26 February, 1785)
39 *Manchester Guardian* (12 November, 1825)
40 Ogden, J. *Manchester A Hundred Years Ago* (1783), p 16
41 *Leeds Mercury* (29 May, 1830)
42 Spiker, S. H. *Travels through England, Wales, and Scotland, in the year 1816*, p 56 et al.
43 Parl History, vol 26 (21 February, 1787), p 492
44 Ibid (12 February, 1787), p 395; Parl Debs, vol 27 (6 June, 1814)
45 'Report from Committee on Woollen Trade Bill, 1803', pp 352, 383
46 'Report of Committee on State of Woollen Manufacture, 1806,' p 7

47 Parl History, vol 25 (20 April, 1785), p 486
48 Ibid, vol 26 (23 February, 1787), p 530
49 *Torrington Diaries*, vol 2, p 160
50 Parl Debs, vol 9 (23 April, 1807), p 533
51 Ibid, vol 37 (19 February, 1818), p 562
52 Hobsbawm, E. J. *The Age of Revolution* (1962), pp 33–8
53 Ogden, J. *Manchester A Hundred Years Ago* (1783), pp 6–7, 84–94
54 Fielden, J. *The Curse of the Factory System* (1836), 1969 ed, p 56
55 Baines, E. *Lancashire* (1824), vol 1, p 113
56 *Leeds Mercury* (21 February, 1824)
57 Howitt, W. *The Rural Life of England* (1838), vol 1, p 259
58 *Nottingham Review* (22 September, 1809)
59 Ibid (3 March, 1815)
60 *Manchester Mercury* (15 October, 1816)
61 Ibid (29 April, 1800)
62 Ibid (19 March, 1805)
63 Spiker, S. H. *Travels through England, Wales, and Scotland, in the year 1816*, pp 72–3
64 *Manchester Guardian* (2 July, 1836)
65 '2nd Report of Commissioners on Children's Employment, 1842', appendix F 17
66 Ashton, T. S. *The Industrial Revolution*, p 17
67 *Torrington Diaries*, vol 2, p 209
68 Quoted by Lord, J. *Capital and Steam Power, 1750–1800* (1923), 1966 ed, p 181
69 *Manchester Guardian* (25 May, 1833)
70 Ibid (4 January, 1834); Howitt, W. *The Rural Life of England, 1838*, vol 1, p 4
71 Parl Debs, 2nd series, vol 12 (25 March, 1825), p 1211
72 Owen, R. *Observations on the Effect of the Manufacturing System* (1815) and *Report to the County of Lanark* (1820)
73 Parl Debs, 3rd series, vol 2 (1 March, 1831), p 1196
74 *Manchester Guardian* (16 April, 1825)
75 Ibid (17 November, 1832)
76 Parl Debs, 2nd series, vol 19 (29 April, 1828), p 216
77 Williams, R. *Culture and Society* (1958), 1961 ed, p 85
78 'Report of Poor Law Commissioners, 1834', appendix A, pp 492, 883
79 Parl Debs, vol 35 (13 March, 1817), pp 1015–16
80 Ibid, 3rd series, vol 8 (11 October, 1831), p 500
81 Gaskell, P. *Artisans and Machinery* (1836), 1968 ed, pp 7, 353

82 *Political Register* (20 November, 1824; 5 February, 1825)
83 'Report from Select Committee on Handloom Weavers' Petitions, 1835, Minutes of Evidence', pp 28–32
84 Porter, G. R. *The Progress of the Nation*, introduction to 1846 ed, p 2
85 Cullen, M. 'Social Statistics in Britain, 1830–52', unpublished Edinburgh PhD thesis (1971), p 45
86 'Report on Petition of Several Weavers, 1811', p 11
87 'Report from Select Committee on Handloom Weavers' Petitions, 1834', p 445
88 'Report from Select Committee on Handloom Weavers' Petitions, 1835, Minutes of Evidence', p 226
89 'Report of Poor Law Commissioners, 1834', Part III, appendix C, p 455
90 *New Statistical Account of Scotland* (1845), vol 6, pp 591–2
91 Parl History, vol 28 (19 April, 1790), p 700
92 'Report from Select Committee on Handloom Weavers' Petitions', p 435
93 Parl History, vol 24 (30 June, 1784), p 1028; vol 25 (20 April, 1785), p 480
94 Ibid, vol 26 (5 February, 1787), p 358
95 Ibid, vol 25 (12 May, 1785), p 585
96 *Leeds Mercury* (24 January, 6 March, 1824)
97 *Nottingham Review* (10 March, 1815)
98 Parl Debs, 2nd series, vol 22 (23 February, 1830), p 866
99 Ibid, 2nd series, vol 24 (28 May, 1830), pp 1223–4; 3rd series, vol 4 (24 June, 1831), pp 337–8

2   The New Land

1 Fielden, J. *The Curse of the Factory System*, p 6
2 'Report of Committee on Woollen Trade Bill, 1803', p 335
3 'Report of Inspector of Factories, July, 1842, L. Horner'
4 Spiker, S. H. *Travels through England, Wales, and Scotland, in the year 1816*, pp 84, 90, 93
5 *Torrington Diaries*, vol 1, p 7; vol 3, pp 154–5
6 Howitt, W. *The Rural Life of England*, vol 2, pp 290–1
7 'Report of Poor Law Commissioners, 1834', appendix A, p 911
8 Howitt, W. *The Rural Life of England*, vol 2, p 286
9 '1st Report of Commissioners on Children's Employment, 1842', appendix, pp 135–6
10 Chambers, J. D. and Mingay, G. E. *The Agricultural Revolution*

(1966), pp 98–104; Hartwell, R. M. 'The Rise of Modern Industry: A Review', in *The Industrial Revolution and Economic Growth* (1971), p 387

11 *Torrington Diaries*, vol 1, p 7; vol 3, pp 154–5
12 *Political Register* (13 April, 1816)
13 Ibid (7 December, 1816)
14 Ibid (20 November, 1824)
15 Howitt, W. *The Rural Life of England*, vol 2, p 112
16 'Report on Petition of Several Weavers, 1811', p 6
17 Coleridge, S. T. *A Lay Sermon*, in White, R. J., ed *Political Tracts of Coleridge, Wordsworth and Shelley* (1953), pp 104–5
18 *New Statistical Account* (1845), vol 6, pp 331, 404
19 *Political Register* (12 July, 1817); *Historical and Literary Tour of a Foreigner in England and Scotland* (1825), vol 2, p 243
20 'Report of Minutes of Evidence before Select Committee on Children's Employment in Manufactories of the United Kingdom, 1816', p 317
21 Cooke Taylor, W. *Notes of a Tour in the Manufacturing Districts of Lancashire* (1842), 1968 ed, p 2
22 Southey, R. *Letters from England* (1807), 1951 ed, p 213
23 *Torrington Diaries*, vol 2, p 23
24 Spiker, S. H. *Travels through England, Wales, and Scotland, in the year 1816*, p 134
25 '2nd Report of Commissioners on State of Large Towns and Populous Districts, 1845', appendix, p 224
26 *Nottingham Journal* (21 December, 1822); Parl Debs, 3rd series, vol 70 (27 June, 1843), p 446
27 Ibid, vol 75 (3 July, 1844), p 285
28 '2nd Report of Commissioners on State of Large Towns and Populous Districts, 1845', appendix, p 184
29 '2nd Report of Commissioners on Children's Employment, 1842', p 33
30 eg Briggs, A. *Victorian Cities* (1968 ed), p 30; Dyos, H. J. (ed) *The Study of Urban History* (1968), pp 359, 171–82
31 *Torrington Diaries*, vol 1, p 184; vol 2, p 23
32 *The Commercial Directory, 1814–15*, Manchester, p 43
33 Spiker, S. H. *Travels through England, Wales, and Scotland, in the year 1816*, pp 69, 95
34 *Historical and Literary Tour of a Foreigner in England and Scotland* (1825), pp 258, 263, preface, pp XII–XIII
35 '1st Report of Commissioners on Children's Employment, 1842', appendix, p 22

36 'Reports from Commissioners on Mining Districts, 1843, S. Staffs.', pp V–VI
37 '1st Report of Commissioners on Children's Employment, 1842', appendix, p 313
38 Ibid, pp 518–19
39 Ibid, pp 135–6
40 Head, Sir George *A Home Tour through the Manufacturing Districts of England, 1835* (1968 ed), pp 130–40
41 *Manchester Mercury* (29 April, 1800)
42 Cooke Taylor, W. *Notes of a Tour in the Manufacturing Districts of Lancashire* (1842), p 54
43 *Manchester Guardian* (9 February, 1822; 27 July, 1833)
44 Ibid (13 September, 1823)
45 '2nd Report of Factories Inquiry Commission, 1833, Medical Reports by Dr Hawkins'
46 Parl Debs, 2nd series, vol 9 (16 June, 1823), p 988
47 Ward, J. T. and Wilson, R. G. *Land and Industry: the landed estate and the industrial revolution* (1971), pp 174–5
48 *Torrington Diaries*, vol 3, pp 81–2
49 Williams, R. *Culture and Society*, p 41

3 The New Society

1 Eden, Sir F. M. *State of the Poor* (1797), p 440
2 Williams, R. *Culture and Society*, p 109
3 *New Statistical Account of Scotland* (1845), vol 7, p 332
4 Wordsworth, W. *The Convention of Cintra*, White, R. J., ed *Political Tracts of Coleridge, Wordsworth and Shelley* (1953), p 187
5 Eliot, G. *Felix Holt* (1907 ed), pp 4–5
6 Gaskell, E. *North and South*, p 376; Briggs, A. *Victorian Cities* (1968 ed), p 268
7 Anderson, M. *Family Structure in Nineteenth Century Lancashire* (1971), ch 5
8 *Torrington Diaries*, vol 3, p 33
9 Parl Debs, vol 41 (9 December, 1819), p 891
10 Ibid, vol 30 (20 March, 1815), p 261
11 'Report from Commissioners on Municipal Corporations, 1835', vol 6, p 134
12 Brontë, C. *Shirley* (1965 ed), p 303
13 '1st Report of Select Committee on Combinations of Workmen, 1838, Minutes of Evidence', p 165
14 *Manchester Guardian* (28 July, 1838)

15 Tobias, J. J. *Crime and Industrial Society in the 19th Century* (1967)
16 Howitt, W. *The Rural Life of England* (1838), vol 1, p 256
17 Gaskell, P. *Artisans and Machinery* (1836), p 124; '4th Report of Select Committee on Poor Law Amendment Act, 1838', p 23
18 *Manchester Mercury* (6 February, 1816); *Manchester Guardian* (21 December, 1836)
19 *Manchester Mercury* (17 December, 1805)
20 *Nottingham Review* (16 August, 1811)
21 'Report of Select Committee on Laws respecting Friendly Societies, 1827', p 40
22 '1st Report of Commissioners on State of Large Towns and Populous Districts, 1844', p VII
23 *Political Register* (9 March, 1811)
24 Ibid (20 November, 1824)
25 Kay, J. P. *The Moral and Physical Condition of the Working Classes,* 1832, p 15
26 'Factory Inquiry Commissioners, Supplementary Report of the Central Board', Part II, C1, The North East
27 Ward, J. T. *The Factory System* (1970), vol 2, p 40
28 Ibid, p 152
29 Galt, J. *Annals of the Parish*, p 274; *Historical and Literary Tour of a Foreigner in England and Scotland* (1825), vol 2, p 70
30 Coleridge, S. T. *A Lay Sermon*, op cit 2:17, p 107
31 Southey, R. *Colloquies on Society* (1824), p 181
32 *Manchester Guardian* (1 April, 1826)
33 Ibid (11 June, 1831)
34 Ibid (22 October, 1835)
35 'Report of Poor Law Commissioners, 1834', appendix A, p 277
36 '1st Report of Select Committee on Poor Law Amendment Act, 1838', p 12; '7th Report', p 5
37 Smith, C. F. 'The Attitude of the Clergy to the Industrial Revolution, as reflected in the First and Second Statistical Accounts', unpublished Glasgow PhD thesis (1953), p 160
38 'Report of Committee on Woollen Trade Bill, 1803', p 67
39 *Torrington Diaries*, vol 3, p 81
40 'Report of Committee on State of Woollen Manufacture, 1806, Minutes of Evidence', p 77
41 'Reports from Assistant Commissioners on Handloom Weavers, 1840-1, Midlands District', p 73
42 Smelser, N. J. *Social Change in the Industrial Revolution* (1959), p 105
43 Fielden, J. *The Curse of the Factory System* (1836), pp 6-7; Parl Debs, vol 30 (15 March, 1815), p 174

44 Gaskell, P. *Artisans and Machinery*, pp 63–5
45 Parl Debs, 3rd series, vol 43 (22 June, 1838), p 969
46 *Leeds Mercury* (30 October, 1830)
47 *Political Register* (20 November, 1824); Cobbett, W. *Rural Rides*, p 394
48 Driver, C. *Tory Radical: Life of Richard Oastler*, p 427
49 Engels, F. *Condition of the Working Class in England*, p 64; Williams, R. *Culture and Society*, pp 41, 86
50 Howitt, W. *The Rural Life of England* (1838), vol 1, p 65; Owen, R. *Report to the County of Lanark* (1820)
51 Cobbett, W. *Rural Rides*, p 273; Williams, R. *Culture and Society*, p 89
52 Parl Debs, 3rd series, vol 24 (13 May, 1830), p 695
53 Head, Sir George *A Home Tour through the Manufacturing Districts of England* (1835), 1968 ed, p 190
54 'Reports of Inspectors of Factories, January, 1837', p 41; '2nd Report of the Commissioners on Children's Employment, 1842', appendix, p D8
55 'Factory Inquiry Commissioners, Supplementary Report of the Central Board', Part II, C1, The North East
56 Driver, C. *Tory Radical: Life of Richard Oastler*, p 61
57 *Leeds Mercury* (30 October, 1830)
58 eg Pollard, S. *The Genesis of Modern Management* (1965), ch 5
59 Kydd, S. H. *History of the Factory Movement* (1857), preface
60 Parl History, vol 32 (12 February, 1796), p 710
61 Parl Debs, vol 30 (11 April, 1815), p 538
62 Ibid, vol 37 (19 February, 1818), p 565; (27 April, 1818), p 342
63 Eden, Sir F. M. *State of the Poor* (1797), pp 420–1
64 *Nottingham Journal* (21 December, 1805)
65 *Manchester Mercury* (4 September, 1810)
66 Kydd, S. H. *The History of the Factory Movement* (1857), p 95
67 Fielden, J. *The Curse of the Factory System* (1836), p 6
68 Southey, R. *Letters from England*, p 208
69 Shelley, P. B. *A Philosophical View of Reform*, White, R. J. op cit 3:4, p 234; Howitt, W. *The Rural Life of England* (1838), vol 1, pp 261–2
70 'Report of the Factory Commissioners, 1833, Mr Powers' Report from Yorkshire', p 74
71 'Report of the Minutes of Evidence before Select Committee on State of Children employed in Manufactories of the United Kingdom, 1816', p 24
72 *Political Register* (20 July, 1833)

73 Ure, A. *The Philosophy of Manufactures* (1835), p 301; *Leeds Mercury* (23 February, 1833); 'Factory Inquiry Commissioners, Supplementary Report of the Central Board', Part II, C1, p 81

74 eg Hill, C. *Reformation to Industrial Revolution*, p 264; Hartwell, R. M. 'Children as Slaves', *The Industrial Revolution and Economic Growth* (1971)

75 'Report of Committee on State of Woollen Manufacture, 1806, Minutes of Evidence', p 440

76 Shelley, P. B. *A Philosophical View of Reform*, op cit 3:4, p 238

77 Axon, W. E. A. *Echoes of Old Lancashire* (1899), pp 112–18

78 'Factory Inquiry Commission, 2nd Report with Minutes of Evidence, Medical Reports by Dr Hawkins'

79 'Report of Factory Commissioners, 1833, Examinations taken by Mr Cowell', p 48

80 Kay, J. P. *The Moral and Physical Condition of the Working Classes* (1832), p 23

81 'Reports of Inspectors of Factories, January, 1837', p 41

82 *Torrington Diaries*, vol 1, p 302

83 *Historical and Literary Tour of a Foreigner in England and Scotland* (1825), vol II, p 258

84 '1st Report of Commissioners on Children's Employment, 1842', appendix, pp 135–6

85 Hart, J. 'Nineteenth Century Social Reform: A Tory Interpretation of History', *Past and Present*, 31 (1967)

86 'Report from Select Committee on Handloom Weavers' Petitions, 1834', p 306

87 '2nd Report of Commissioners on Children's Employment, 1842', appendix, p F22

88 *Political Register* (31 July, 1813)

89 Howitt, W. *The Rural Life of England* (1838), vol 1, p 286

90 Galt, J. *Annals of the Parish*, p 179

91 Flinn, M. W. *Chadwick's Report on the Sanitary Condition of the Labouring Population of Great Britain, 1842* (1965), introduction

92 '1st Report of the Commissioners on Children's Employment, 1842', appendix, p 350; Smith, C. F. 'The Attitude of the Clergy to the Industrial Revolution as reflected in the First and Second Statistical Accounts', unpublished Glasgow PhD thesis (1953), p 96

93 'Report on the Sanitary Condition of the Labouring Population of Great Britain by Edwin Chadwick, 1842, Local Reports, Leeds', p 409

94 Howitt, W. *The Rural Life of England* (1838), vol 1, p 257; Gaskell, P. *Artisans and Machinery*, p 22

95 *Political Register* (20 November, 1824; 15 December, 1827)

96 '2nd Report of Commissioners on Children's Employment', appendix, pp c69–70

97 *Torrington Diaries*, vol 2, p 205; *Commercial Directory, 1816–17*, p 6

98 *Manchester Mercury* (14 February, 1815); *New Statistical Account of Scotland*, vol 11, p 85

99 Harrison, J. F. C. *The Early Victorians* (1971), pp 70–2

100 *Manchester Mercury* (25 September, 1800)

101 Parl Debs, 3rd series, vol 11 (16 March, 1832), p 349

102 Laslett, P. *The World We Have Lost*, pp 142–4

103 Gaskell, P. *Artisans and Machinery*, p 253

104 '1st Report from Select Committee on Combinations of Workmen and Minutes of Evidence, 1888', p 165

105 Best, G. F. *Mid-Victorian Britain, 1851–75* (1971), p 192

106 '2nd Report of Commissioners on Children's Employment, 1842', p 204

107 *Manchester Guardian* (19 December, 1835)

108 '2nd Report of Commissioners on Children's Employment, 1842', appendix Q9

109 Ibid, Q 28–9

110 Ibid, F131–2; *Manchester Guardian* (23 February, 1833)

111 Kay, J. P. *The Moral and Physical Condition of the Working Classes* (1832), pp 4–5

112 Fielden, J. *The Curse of the Factory System* (1836), p 76

113 Parl Debs, 3rd series, vol 55 (4 August, 1840), pp 1277–8

114 'Reports from Commissioners on Mining Districts, 1843, S. Staffs', p XIX

115 Ibid, '1844, Scotland and parts of Staffs.', pp 16–17

116 Disraeli, B. *Sybil* (Penguin ed), p 67

117 Coleridge, S. T. *A Lay Sermon*, op cit 2:17, p 103

118 Shelley, P. B. *A Philosophical View of Reform*, op cit 3:4, p 237

119 *Political Register* (18 April, 1812)

120 Hammond, J. L. and Barbara *Rise of Modern Industry* (1966 ed), p 205

121 Parl Debs, vol 35 (11 February, 1817), pp 321 et al

122 *Manchester Mercury* (14, 21 June, 1808)

123 *Manchester Guardian* (15, 22 October, 1831)

124 Brontë, C. *Shirley*, p 107

125 *Manchester Guardian* (30 October, 1830)

126 Kay, J. P. *The Moral and Physical Condition of the Working Classes* (1832), p 10; *Nottingham Journal* (14 March, 1834)
127 Parl Debs, 3rd series, vol 22 (26 March, 1834), p 728
128 Ure, A. *The Philosophy of Manufactures*, pp 41, 279
129 '1st Report of Select Committee on Combinations of Workmen and Minutes of Evidence, 1838', pp 130–1
130 Parl Debs, vol 37 (10 April, 1818), pp 1260–1
131 'Reports from Assistant Commissioners on Handloom Weavers, 1840–1, Midlands District', p 188; '1st Report of Commissioners on Children's Employment, 1842', appendix, p 405; Ibid, p 518; 'Reports of Commissioners on Mining Districts, 1844, Scotland and parts of Staffs.', p 16
132 Disraeli, B. *Sybil*, p 222
133 'Report of Poor Law Commissioners, 1834', appendix C, p 457c
134 'Reports from Assistant Commissioners on Handloom Weavers, 1840–1, Midlands District', p 188
135 Parl Debs, vol 41 (9 December, 1819), p 916
136 'Report of the Poor Law Commissioners, 1834', appendix C, p 111c
137 '1st Report of Commissioners on Children's Employment, 1842', appendix, p 201
138 Ibid, p 313
139 Ibid, pp 518–19; 'Reports from Commissioners on Mining Districts, 1843, S. Staffs.', p V
140 Ibid, '1844, Scotland and parts of Staffs.', p 28
141 Shelley, P. B. *A Philosophical View of Reform*, op cit 3:4, p 204
142 Cobbett, W. *Rural Rides*, p 406; Williams, R. *Culture and Society*, p 86
143 '1st Report of Commissioners on Children's Employment, 1842', appendix, p 201
144 Spiker, S. H. *Travels through England, Wales, and Scotland, in the year 1816*, vol 2, p 80
145 Cooke Taylor, W. *Notes of a Tour in the Manufacturing Districts of Lancashire* (1842), p 164; Engels, F. *Condition of the Working Classes in England*, p 56
146 Briggs, A. *Victorian Cities*, pp 89–90
147 Ibid, p 88, ch 5; Pollard, S. *A History of Labour in Sheffield*, pp 41–2; Barker, T. C. and Harris, J. R. *A Merseyside Town in the Industrial Revolution, St. Helens, 1750–1900* (1959), pp 288, 412; Foster, J. '18th Century Towns—A Class Dimension', in Dyos, H. J. (ed), *The Study of Urban History*, pp 281–99

148 Gatrell, V. A. C., introduction to Owen, R. *A New View of Society* (1970), p 47
149 *Political Register* (7 December, 1833)
150 Howitt, W. *The Rural Life of England* (1838), vol 1, p 145
151 Engels, F. *Condition of the Working Class in England*, p 273
152 Disraeli, B. *Sybil*, p 67
153 Shelley, P. B. *A Philosophical View of Reform*, op cit 3:4, p 235
154 *Political Register* (10 July, 20 November, 1824)
155 Gaskell, E. *North and South*, p 125
156 *Manchester Guardian* (25 May, 1833)
157 'Report from Select Committee on Handloom Weavers' Petitions, 1834', p 12
158 'Reports from Assistant Commissioners on Handloom Weavers, 1840–1, Midlands District', p 193
159 Erickson, C. *British Industrialists, 1850–1950; Steel and Hosiery* (1959)
160 *Manchester Mercury* (3 June, 1806); Parl Debs, 3rd series, vol 2 (1 March, 1831), pp 1141–2
161 *Manchester Guardian* (5 June, 1830)
162 Eliot, G. *Felix Holt*, p 66
163 Parl History, vol 25 (20 April, 1785), p 483
164 *Manchester Guardian* (15 October, 1831)
165 *Nottingham Review* (25 June, 1813)
166 *Manchester Guardian* (22 January, 2 March, 1822; 1 February, 1823)
167 Parl Debs, 2nd series, vol 1 (3 May, 1820), pp 72–3
168 Ibid, vol 5 (9 April, 1821), p 89
169 *Leeds Mercury* (16 January, 1830)
170 Parl Debs, vol 37 (16 March, 1837), p 588
171 Ward, J. T. and Wilson, R. G. (ed) *Land and Industry* (1971), p 10
172 Parl Debs, vol 29 (17 February, 1815), p 835
173 Ibid, 3rd series, vol 37 (16 March, 1837), p 594
174 eg Ibid, vol 75 (25 June, 1844), p 1407
175 *Manchester Guardian* (5, 26 January, 1839)
176 Parl Debs, vol 29 (17 February, 1815), p 826; vol 30 (6 March, 1815), p 20; vol 31 (6 June, 1815), p 119
177 *Leeds Mercury* (1 May, 1824)
178 Parl Debs, 2nd series, vol 22 (23 February, 1830), p 860
179 Parl Debs, vol 6 (14 March, 1806), p 433
180 *Manchester Guardian* (24 January, 1846)

181 'Reports from Assistant Commissioners on Handloom Weaving, 1840–1, Midlands District', p 193
182 'Report of Constabulary Commissioners, 1839', p 181
183 Brougham, H. *Life and Times*, vol 2, 1871 (1972 ed), pp 342–3
184 Coats, A. W., ed. Jones and Mingay 'The Classical Economists and the Labourer', in *Land, Labour, and Population* (1967), pp 109–110
185 Cooke Taylor, W. *Notes of a Tour in the Manufacturing Districts of Lancashire* (1842), pp 6–7

4   The New Values

1 Parl Debs, 2nd series, vol 9 (14 May, 1823)
2 *Manchester Guardian* (26 January, 1822)
3 Parl History, vol 32 (12 February, 1796), pp 706–10
4 Driver, C. *Tory Radical: The Life of Richard Oastler* (1946), p 432
5 'Report of Poor Law Commissioners, 1833', appendix C, p 455c
6 Taylor, A. J. *Laissez-Faire and State Intervention in Nineteenth Century Britain* (1972), pp 27–9
7 'Report from Committee on Silk Ribbon Weavers' Petitions, 1818', p 52
8 'Report of Committee on State of Woollen Manufacture, 1806', p 12
9 *Manchester Guardian* (16 March, 1822)
10 Parl Debs, vol 37 (27 April, 1818), p 345; (16 February, 1818), p 441
11 Ibid, vol 33 (3 April, 1816), p 886
12 Taylor, A. J. *Laissez-Faire and State Intervention in Nineteenth Century Britain*, pp 42–4
13 *Leeds Mercury* (29 May, 1824)
14 '15th Report of Select Committee on Poor Law Amendment Act, 1838', appendix A, p 27
15 'Report of Committee on Cotton Weavers' Petitions, 1803', p 6
16 Parl Debs, vol 11 (19 May, 1808), pp 425–8
17 'Report from Select Committee on Handloom Weavers' Petitions, 1834', p 391; *Manchester Guardian* (20 June, 1835)
18 Ibid (21 January, 1832; 28 February, 1824)
19 Parl Debs, vol 5 (27 May, 1805), p 118; *Leeds Mercury* (29 May, 1824)

20 'Report on Petition of Several Weavers, 1811', p 2
21 'Report of Poor Law Commissioners, 1834', appendix A, Part 1, p 602
22 Kay, J. P. *The Moral and Physical Condition of the Working Classes* (1832), p 45
23 Taylor, A. J. *Laissez-Faire and State Intervention in Nineteenth Century Britain*, pp 44–5
24 *Leeds Mercury* (30 October, 1830)
25 'Report of Committee on State of Woollen Manufacture, 1806', p 3
26 Parl Debs, 2nd series, vol 1 (3 May, 1820), p 191
27 *Leeds Mercury* (30 January, 1830)
28 Parl Debs, vol 30 (10 March, 1815), p 117
29 Parl History, vol 25 (8 July, 1785), p 857
30 *Manchester Mercury* (18 February, 1800; 22 February, 1803; 24 January, 1815; 23 May, 1815)
31 Church, R. A. and Chapman, S. D. 'Gravener Henson and the Making of the English Working Class', *Land, Labour, and Population in the Industrial Revolution* (1967), ed Jones and Mingay, p 153
32 Taylor, A. J. *Laissez-Faire and State Intervention in Nineteenth Century Britain*, p 41
33 Parl Debs, vol 2 (6 July, 1804), p 744
34 *Manchester Guardian* (25 April, 1846)
35 Parl Debs, 3rd series, vol 8 (11 October, 1831), p 501
36 Cobbett, W. *Rural Rides*, p 395
37 Southey, R. *Colloquies on Society* (1824), 1887 ed, p 183
38 Driver, C. *Tory Radical: The Life of Richard Oastler*, p 430
39 Ibid, p 432
40 Southey, R. *Letters from England* (1807), 1951 ed, p 209
41 Coleridge, S. T. *A Lay Sermon*, op cit 2:17, pp 80, 101, 106
42 Wordsworth, 'The Convention of Cintra', White, R. J., op cit 3:4, p 183
43 Williams, R. *Culture and Society*, p 42
44 Ibid, p 109
45 Ibid, p 87
46 Ibid, p 72
47 Howitt, W. *The Rural Life of England* (1838), vol 2, pp 110–11
48 Ruskin, J. *The Two Paths* (1859)
49 Bamford, S. *Early Days* (1967 ed), p 122
50 Driver, C. *Tory Radical: The Life of Richard Oastler*, p 432
51 Southey, R. *Colloquies on Society* (1824), p 183

52 Gaskell, E. *Mary Barton* (1966), Panther ed, p 374
53 Fielden, J. *The Curse of the Factory System* (1836), p 48
54 Quoted by Toynbee, A. *The Industrial Revolution* (1884), 1969 ed, p 194
55 *Manchester Mercury* (23 September, 1800)
56 *Manchester Guardian* (24 May, 1823)
57 Parl Debs, 2nd series (26 April, 1821), pp 1316–19
58 'Reports of Assistant Commissioners on Handloom Weavers, 1840–1, Midlands District', p 193
59 'Report of Commissioners on Mining Districts 1844, Scotland and parts of Staffs.', p 32
60 '1st Report of Poor Law Commissioners, 1834', appendix A, p 385 A
61 Henson, G. and White, G. *A Few Remarks on the State of the Laws at Present in Existence for Regulating Masters and Workpeople* (1823), pp 140–1
62 Kingsley, C. *Alton Locke* (1884 ed), p 338
63 Driver, C. *Tory Radical: The Life of Richard Oastler*, p 426
64 Toynbee, A. *The Industrial Revolution*, p 193
65 Ibid, p 93
66 '1st Report of Poor Law Commissioners, 1834', appendix A, p 500
67 Gaskell, E. *North and South*, p 108
68 Cobbett, W. *Rural Rides*, p 316
69 Williams, R. *Culture and Society*, p 106
70 Ibid, p 45
71 Parl Debs, 3rd series, vol 17 (3 April, 1883), p 105
72 *Manchester Guardian* (27 February, 1830)
73 Southey, R. *Letters from England*, p 210
74 *Political Register* (27 October, 1804)
75 Shelley, P. B. *A Philosophical View of Reform*, op cit 3:4, pp 238–9; *A Defence of Poetry*, p 205
76 Driver, C. *Tory Radical: The Life of Richard Oastler*, p 136; Kydd, S. H. *History of the Factory Movement*, p 92
77 Thompson, W. 'Labour Rewarded' (1827), Cole, G. D. H. and Filson, A. W. *British Working Class Movements, 1787–1875* (1967 ed), p 206
78 Kydd, S. H. *History of the Factory Movement*, vol 2, p 100; Driver, C. *Tory Radical: The Life of Richard Oastler*, p 433
79 Ibid, p 426
80 '21st Report of Poor Law Commissioners, 1834', p 5
81 Howitt, W. *The Rural Life of England* (1838), vol 1, p 259

82 Driver, C. *Tory Radical: The Life of Richard Oastler*, p 431; Taylor, A. J. *Laissez-Faire and State Intervention in Nineteenth Century Britain*, p 28

83 Ibid

84 '1st Report of Poor Law Commissioners, 1834', appendix A, p 279

85 'Report of Select Committee on Health of Towns, 1840', pp IV, IX

86 'Report on Sanitary Condition of the Labour Population of Great Britain, 1842, by Edwin Chadwick', p 279

87 '2nd Report of Commissioners on State of Large Towns and Populous Districts, 1844, Lancashire', pp 72–3

88 Open University *The Debate on Industrialisation* (1971), p 23

89 Driver, C. *Tory Radical: The Life of Richard Oastler*, p 296

90 '21st Report of Select Committee on Poor Law Amendment Act, 1838', p 5

91 Taylor, A. J. *Laissez-Faire and State Intervention in Nineteenth Century Britain*, pp 36, 44

5 The Search for the Past

1 Parl Debs, vol 2 (13 June, 1804), p 669

2 'Report of Committee on State of Woollen Manufacture, 1806', pp 445–8

3 Parl Debs, vol 35 (13 March, 1817), p 1053

4 Ibid, vol 41 (9 December, 1819), p 916

5 'Reports from Assistant Commissioners on Handloom Weavers, 1839', pp 5, 461, 536

6 'Reports from Commissioners on Framework knitters, 1845, Notts.', pp 29, 242

7 Smith, C. F. 'The Attitude of the Clergy to the Industrial Revolution, as reflected in the First and Second Statistical Accounts', unpublished Glasgow PhD thesis (1953), p 146

8 'Reports from Assistant Commissioners on Handloom Weavers, 1839', pp 216–18; Williams, R. *Culture and Society*, p 100

9 *Manchester Mercury* (30 September, 1800); Cobbett, W. *Rural Rides*, pp 394–5

10 *Political Register* (14 September, 1816)

11 Smelser, N. J. *Social Change in the Industrial Revolution*, p 185

12 'Report of Select Committee on Handloom Weavers' Petitions, 1834', pp 53, 61, 117; 'Report of Commissioners on Handloom Weavers, 1841', p 39

13 *Nottingham Review* (12 June, 1918); Felkin, W. *History of the Machine-Wrought Hosiery and Lace Manufactures* (1867), pp 117, 239
14 Dodd, W. *The Factory System Illustrated* (1842), 1968 ed, p 199
15 Brontë, C. *Shirley*, p 511
16 Dodd, W. *The Factory System Illustrated*, p 311
17 *Torrington Diaries*, vol 3, pp 148, 155
18 *Political Register* (31 July, 1813)
19 Howitt, W. *The Rural Life of England* (1838), vol 1, p 183; vol 2, pp 138–41, 286, 306–7
20 Williams, R. *Culture and Society*, p 139
21 Gatrell, V. A. C., introduction to Owen, R. *A New View of Society*, pp 44–5, 50
22 Howitt, W. *The Rural Life of England* (1838), vol 1, p 141; Coleridge, S. T. *A Lay Sermon*, op cit 2:17, p 110
23 Disraeli, B. *Sybil*, p 223
24 Cobbett, W. *Rural Rides*, pp 254, 226–7, 495–6
25 Williams, R. *Culture and Society*, p 95
26 Disraeli, B. *Sybil*, p 171
27 Disraeli, B. *Coningsby*, p 111
28 Gatrell, V. A. C., introduction to Owen, R. *A New View of Society*, p 50
29 Driver, C. *Tory Radical: Life of Richard Oastler*, p 136
30 Brontë, C. *Shirley*, p 106
31 Toynbee, A. *The Industrial Revolution*, p 191
32 Cobbett, W. *Rural Rides*, pp 394–5
33 *Political Register* (20 November, 1824)
34 Kydd, S. H. *History of the Factory Movement*, p 10
35 Gaskell, P. *Artisans and Machinery*, pp 12–14
36 Pollard, S. *The Genesis of Modern Management* (1965), 1968 ed, p 192
37 'Report of Committee on Woollen Trade Bill, 1803, and Committee on State of Woollen Manufacture, 1806'
38 Ure, A. *The Philosophy of Manufactures*, p 334
39 Prest, J. *The Industrial Revolution in Coventry* (1960), p 72
40 Williams, R. *Culture and Society*, p 108
41 Hartwell, R. M. 'Interpretations of the Industrial Revolution in England', *Industrial Revolution and Economic Growth* (1971), p 388; Williams, R. *The Country and the City*, p 37
42 'Report of the Poor Law Commissioners, 1834', appendix C, p 453c
43 Parl Debs, 3rd series, vol 8 (11 October, 1831), p 501

44 Williams, R. *Culture and Society*, p 34
45 Gaskell, P. *Artisans and Machinery*, p 46
46 Driver, C. *Tory Radical: The Life of Richard Oastler*, pp 296–7
47 *Political Register* (23 November, 1811)
48 'Report of Poor Law Commissioners, 1834', appendix C, pp 453c, 461c
49 Pollard, S. 'Nineteenth Century Co-operation; From Community building to Shop-keeping', Briggs and Saville (ed) *Essays in Labour History* (1960), 1967 ed, pp 97–8
50 Cole, G. D. H. and Filson, A. W. *British Working Class Movements, 1789–1875*, pp 424, 432, 433
51 Ibid, pp 371–2, 398–401; MacAskill, J. 'The Chartist Land Plan', Briggs, A. (ed), *Chartist Studies* (1969)
52 Disraeli, B. *Coningsby*, p 111

6   Reform and Reconciliation

1 Ward, J. T. and Wilson, R. G. *Land and Industry*, p 11
2 Richards, E. S. *Leviathan of Wealth* (1973), pp 18, 184–5
3 Ward, J. T. and Wilson, R. G. *Land and Industry*, pp 10–11, 29, 32
4 Ibid, p 53
5 Hobsbawm, E. J. *Industry and Empire*, p 62
6 Kitson Clark, G. 'The Repeal of the Corn Laws and the Politics of the Forties', *Economic History Review*, 2nd series, 4 (1951–2)
7 Hobsbawm, E. J. *Industry and Empire*, p 64
8 Williams, R. *Culture and Society*, p 110
9 Ibid, pp 33, 91
10 Webb, B. *My Apprenticeship* (1926), 1971 ed, p 191
11 Ibid, p 347; Engels, F. *The Condition of the Working Class in England*, p 12
12 Williams, R. *The Country and the City*, p 231
13 *Manchester Guardian* (5 June, 1830)
14 Ibid (5 October, 1833)
15 'Reports from Commissioners on Mining Districts, 1843, S. Staffs.', p XXII; Ibid, '1844, Scotland and parts of Staffs.', p 17
16 Parl Debs, 3rd series, vol 51 (4 February, 1840), p 1225
17 Ibid, vol 77 (18 February, 1845), pp 653–6
18 Williams, R. *Culture and Society*, p 106
19 Gaskell, E. *Mary Barton*, p 375

20 Gaskell, E. *North and South*, p 525
21 'Reports from Commissioners on Mining Districts, 1845, Parts of Scotland and Yorkshire', p 22
22 Lovett, W. *Autobiography* (1876), 1920 ed, p 415
23 Brontë, C. *Shirley*, p 108
24 Williams, R. *Culture and Society*, p 92
25 Parl Debs, 3rd series, vol 85 (13 May, 1846)
26 *Leeds Mercury* (16 October, 1830)
27 'Report of Poor Law Commissioners, 1834', appendix A, Part II, p 211a
28 *Leeds Mercury* (29 October, 1831)
29 Briggs, A. *Victorian Cities*, p 145
30 Fielden, J. *The Curse of the Factory System*, p 38
31 Kydd, S. H. *History of the Factory Movement*, p 29
32 '2nd Report of Commissioners on State of Large Towns and Populous Districts, 1845', appendix, 'Dr L. Playfair on Large Towns in Lancashire', pp 72–3
33 'Report of Select Committee on Health of Towns, 1840', p XIV; 'Reports from Commissioners on Mining Districts, 1845, Parts of Scotland and Yorkshire', p 6
34 Williams, R. *Culture and Society*, p 40
35 Parl Debs, 3rd series, vol 31 (16 March, 1837), p 600
36 '1st Report of Commissioners on Children's Employment, 1842', appendix, p 352
37 Parl Debs, 3rd series, vol 85 (22 May, 1846), pp 1033–44
38 Ibid, vol 37 (16 March, 1837), p 600
39 Kay, J. P. *The Moral and Physical Condition of the Working Classes* (1832), p 10
40 Parl Debs, vol 33 (3 April, 1816)
41 Fielden, J. *The Curse of the Factory System*, p 28; Coleridge, S. T. *A Lay Sermon*, op cit 2:17, p 115
42 Parl Debs, 3rd series, vol 79 (8 April, 1845), pp 335–6
43 Kay, J. P. *The Moral and Physical Condition of the Working Classes* (1832), p 10
44 Porter, G. R. *The Progress of the Nation*, preface to 2nd ed, 1846
45 'Report on Sanitary Condition of the Labouring Population of Great Britain by Edwin Chadwick, 1842', p 279
46 *Manchester Guardian* (7 March, 1846); Parl Debs, 3rd series, vol 91 (19 March, 1847), p 644
47 Parl Debs, 3rd series, vol 66 (14 February, 1843), p 575; vol 76 (30 July, 1844), p 1566
48 Ibid, vol 85 (13 May, 1846), p 504

49 *Manchester Guardian* (24 August, 1833)
50 Parl Debs, 3rd series, vol 57 (11 March, 1841), p 130; vol 51 (4 February, 1840), pp 1235-6
51 Porter, G. R. *Progress of the Nation*, preface to 2nd ed, 1846
52 Howitt, W. *The Rural Life of England*, vol 2, pp 273, 150
53 '2nd Report of Commissioners on Children's Employment, 1842', appendix F38
54 *Manchester Guardian* (24 January, 1824)
55 Williams, R. *Culture and Society*, p 123
56 Cullen, M. J. 'Social Statistics in Britain, 1830-52', unpublished Edinburgh PhD thesis (1971), p 425
57 Parl Debs, 3rd series, vol 20 (29 July, 1833), p 143
58 'Reports of Assistant Commissioners on Handloom Weavers, 1840-1, Midlands District'
59 '2nd Report of Commissioners on Children's Employment', appendix, Part 11, 07; *Manchester Guardian* (26 January, 1833)
60 Kay, J. P. *The Moral and Physical Condition of the Working Classes*, p 97
61 Ure, A. *The Philosophy of Manufactures*, pp 326, 372
62 Parl Debs, 3rd series, vol 20 (29 July, 1833), pp 139-43
63 'Reports of Commissioners on Mining Districts, 1850, S. Staffs.'
64 *Political Register* (29 May, 1830)
65 Engels, F. *The Condition of the Working Class in England*, p 271
66 'Report of Select Committee on Handloom Weavers, 1834', p 309
67 'Reports of Commissioners on Mining Districts, 1843, S. Staffs.', p CXXIV
68 *Life of Thomas Cooper*, by himself, p 393
69 Williams, R. *Culture and Society*, p 161
70 *Manchester Guardian* (26 December, 1835)
71 Harrison, R. *Before the Socialists* (1965), p 114
72 eg Perkin, H. J. *The Origins of Modern English Society, 1780-1880*, p 381 et al
73 Ibid, p 356; Ure, A. *The Philosophy of Manufactures*, pp 425-8
74 Perkin, H. J. *The Origins of Modern English Society*, pp 354-64
75 'Report of Select Committee on Friendly Societies Bill, 1849', p iii
76 Pollard, S. 'Nineteenth Century Co-operation; From Community Building to Shopkeeping', Briggs and Saville (ed) *Essays in Labour History* (1960), 1967 ed, pp 74-113
77 Ibid

78 Hobsbawm, E. J. 'The Labour Aristocracy in Nineteenth-century Britain', *Labouring Men* (1968 ed), pp 272–316
79 Dyos, H. J. (ed) *The Study of Urban History* (1968), p 278

7 The Industrial Revolution and the Historians

1 eg Wrigley, E. A. *Population and History* (1969); Armstrong, A. *Stability and Change in an English County Town* (1974)
2 eg Ward, J. T. and Wilson, R. G. *Land and Industry: the landed estate and the industrial revolution* (1971)
3 Laslett, Peter *The World We Have Lost* (1965)
4 Hammond, J. L. and Barbara *The Town Labourer* (1917), 1966 ed, p 26
5 Chambers, J. D. and Mingay, G. E. *The Agricultural Revolution, 1750–1880* (1966), pp 98–104
6 Hill, C. *Reformation to Industrial Revolution* (1967), 1969 ed, p 272
7 Hartwell, R. M. 'Children as Slaves', *The Industrial Revolution and Economic Growth* (1971)
8 Hill, C. *Reformation to Industrial Revolution*, p 264
9 The factory debate can be sampled from Hutt, W. M. 'The Factory System of the Early 19th Century', Hayek, F. A. (ed) *Capitalism and the Historians* (1954); Hobsbawm, E. J. 'History and "The Dark Satanic Mills" ', *Labouring Men* (1964)
10 Hutt, W. M. 'The Factory System of the Early 19th Century', op cit; Hartwell, R. M. 'The Rise of Modern Industry', *The Industrial Revolution and Economic Growth* (1971)
11 McDonagh, O. *A pattern of government growth, 1800–60: the passenger acts and their enforcement* (1961)
12 Hart, J. 'Nineteenth Century Social Reform: A Tory Interpretation of History', *Past and Present*, 31 (1965). This contains a summary and critique of the new ideas
13 Thompson, E. P. *The Making of the English Working Class* (1963)
14 For an outstanding contribution to this debate see Foster, John *Class struggle and the industrial revolution* (1974)
15 eg Wearmouth, R. F. *Methodism and the Working Class Movements of England, 1800–50*; Hobsbawm, E. J. 'Methodism and the threat of Revolution in Britain', *Labouring Men* (1964); Thompson, E. P. *The Making of the English Working Class* (1963), ch 11
16 eg Perkin, Harold *The Origins of Modern English Society, 1780–1880* (1969), ch 5 gives a balanced view

17 eg Hartwell, R. M. 'The Rising Standard of Living in England, 1800–1850', *Economic History Review*, vol 13, no 3 (1961)
18 Thompson, E. P. *The Making of the English Working Class* (1968 ed), pp 485–6. In recent years E. J. Hobsbawm, Christopher Hill, and E. P. Thompson have joined the Webbs, the Hammonds, the Coles, and Tawney in fulfilling this double role
19 Hammond, J. L. and Barbara *The Town Labourer*, pp 28, 47, 102–3, 108, 143
20 Clapham, J. H. *An Economic History of Modern Britain: The Railway Age* (1926), pp 548–65
21 eg Hobsbawm, E. J. 'The British Standard of Living, 1790–1850', and 'The Standard of Living Debate: A Postscript', *Labouring Men* (1964)
22 Taylor, A. J. 'Progress and Poverty in Britain, 1780–1850', *History*, 153 (1960), discusses some of these issues
23 Ibid, for an attempt to explore the common ground
24 Hartwell, R. M. 'The Standard of Living Controversy: A Summary', Hartwell, R. M. (ed) *The Industrial Revolution* (1970)

Index